A Lincoln.

ABRAHAM LINCOLN:

His Life and Public Services.

BY

MRS. P. A. HANAFORD,

AUTHOR OF "OUR MARTYRED PRESIDENT," "THE YOUNG CAPTAIN," ETC.

"That life is long which answers life's great end." — YOUNG.

"God buries his workmen, but carries on the work." — CHARLES WESLEY.

"The righteous hath hope in his death." — PROV. xiv. 32.

BOSTON:
B. B. RUSSELL AND COMPANY.
S. S. BOYDEN, CHICAGO, ILL.
1866.

PRINTED BY
GEO. C. RAND & AVERY.

TO

ALL LOYAL MEN AND WOMEN,

NORTH AND SOUTH, EAST AND WEST,

TO

THE UNION ARMY AND NAVY,

AND ESPECIALLY

TO THE LONG-OPPRESSED RACE FOR WHOM

President Lincoln

WROTE

THE EMANCIPATION PROCLAMATION,

THIS RECORD OF HIS STAINLESS LIFE AND

MARTYR'S DEATH IS NOW

INSCRIBED.

PREFACE.

It has been thought that a biography of our martyred President, brief yet comprehensive, and published in a style which would bring it within the limits of all who would buy any volume, ought to be published at once.

Of this remarkable man it can be said, as it was said of our Lord Jesus Christ, "The common people heard him gladly;" and therefore a memoir expressly designed for the mass of readers in our country cannot fail to be warmly welcomed.

There will doubtless be many biographies of our late President, written by different pens, and of varying size, style, and merit. But the field is open to all; and no one has a right to monopolize it, and thus prohibit others from labor in the same direction. Every new book finds new readers, and meets some unsupplied demand. If a volume, like this now offered, be indeed — as it is supposed to be — a *desideratum*, its own readers, for whom it is designed, will cluster about it, and the hopes of its author and publisher be realized.

The special aim of this volume is twofold: First, To present a truthful picture of the character of the great and good man who has fallen among us; delineating, as far as possible in narrating the events of his life, the growth and development of those grand and heroic virtues which stamp him with the unmistakable seal of Heaven's approval, and make his name

> "One of the few, the *immortal* names
> That were not born to die."

And, secondly, To show that "the course of human events" was such, during his earthly existence, and his relation to them so peculiar in the providence of God, as to indicate that he was specially commissioned for his day and work, — a man *of* the times, and a man *for* the times; that he lived long enough to be able to say, like his Lord, "It is finished," and then passed on to hear from divine lips the unrivalled words of welcome, "Well done, good and faithful servant! enter thou into the joy of thy Lord!"

Should this volume deepen the convictions of its readers in the grand truths of God's sovereignty on earth as well as in heaven, and of his love to all the family of man, shown especially in his care for the outcast and oppressed; and should it make them love freedom and righteousness more and more, as they contemplate the character and life of the Martyr-President, — the labor spent in its preparation will not have been in vain, and to God will be ascribed the glory.

P. A. H.

READING, MASS.

CONTENTS.

CHAPTER X.

CHAPTER XI.

CHAPTER XII.

ABRAHAM LINCOLN.

CHAPTER I.

EARLY DAYS IN OBSCURITY.

"Honor and shame from no condition rise:
Act well your part,—there all the honor lies."
POPE.

"But God hath chosen the foolish things of the world to confound the wise; and God hath chosen the weak things of the world to confound the things that are mighty;

"And base things of the world, and things which are despised, hath God chosen, yea, and things which are not, to bring to nought things that are:

"That no flesh should glory in his presence."—ST. PAUL (1 Cor. i. 27).

THE sixteenth President of the United States was born in obscurity. No Gabriel heralded his birth; no shepherds saw the star of his nativity, and heard the chanting of celestial visitants to earth; nor did sages and philosophers come to his cradle-side with costly offerings and significant homage. Yet he had a grand mission on earth to perform, and was to be, in some sense, the savior of many, and in the obscurity of his birth, at least, resembled the Master whose footsteps he afterward loved to follow. It is the design of Infinite Wisdom that the tiny acorn should precede the towering oak, the little rivulet commence the mighty river; and that Wisdom was no less manifest in the humble birth and parentage of one whom the good of all nations, in all time, should afterward delight to honor.

In that part of Hardin County, Ky., now known as La Rue, on the 12th of February, 1809, ABRAHAM

LINCOLN entered upon existence. His father, Thomas Lincoln, and the grandfather whose patriarchal name he bore, were natives of Rockingham County, Va., a part of the "Old Dominion" to which their ancestors had removed from Berks County, Penn.

Abraham, the grandfather, migrated to Kentucky with his family in the year 1780, where he obtained possession of a small tract of land in the then wilderness, and there erected a rude cabin, and commenced a life of toil and danger. Like the Pilgrim colonists of our own New England, he was accustomed to carry his gun with his axe, or other implement of labor, when he went forth to his toil; and, when he laid his head upon his nightly pillow, it was with his trusty firelock conveniently at hand, that there might be safety for him and his should the wild war-whoop of the savage Indian break upon his slumbers. These merciless "lords of the forest" manifested intense hostility to the "pale-faces," and with ruthless barbarity murdered men, women, and children, when the opportunity was afforded them. For four years, our President's grandfather was unharmed; but at the end of that period, while he was using his axe at a place some four miles from his home, he was suddenly attacked by the Indians, and, unable to reach his gun in season, was overpowered, killed, and scalped after the hideous Indian fashion. Search was made for him when his prolonged absence awakened alarm, and the next morning his remains were discovered. This loss of their beloved father resulted finally in the scattering of the children.

The father of our martyred President left his early home when only about twelve years old, but afterwards returned to Kentucky, and in 1806 married Miss Nancy Sparrow, who was a native of Virginia. Both of our late President's parents were members of the Baptist Church, and well known as a pious, unassuming, but uneducated couple. The father could neither read nor write, save to scribble his name in rude hieroglyphic letters which could hardly be understood. The mother could not write, but she could read; and this accomplishment made her seem a remarkable woman for that time and place. Moreover, it gave her the power to peruse the blessed volume, and to read its holy words to her husband for his guidance and consolation, and its interesting stories to her beloved son Abraham.

Thomas Lincoln appreciated this privilege which his wife possessed, and it deepened his respect for her; for, though himself so unlearned, he appreciated all the more, perhaps, the advantages of education: and all who possessed a more than ordinary share of learning challenged and received from him the most unbounded respect. And, could he have foreseen the career of his noble and excellent son, he would have been still more desirous than he was that Abraham should have the opportunity to study, and still more proud of the facility with which he mastered his lessons.

It was at the age of seven that "Abe," as he was familiarly termed in the home-circle, first began to attend school in a small academy with a teacher who loved not his great work, and was only anxious that his pupils should learn to read and write. Having put into their hands the power to do these two great things, he left them to use that power or not, as they pleased. But, under this apathetic and incompetent teacher, Abraham was not destined long to stay.

His father was a lover of liberty. He could not breathe freely in a slave State. He saw the peculiar disadvantages of life for poor whites in a land where labor was degraded by slavery; and he resolved that his children should be relieved from his own unsatisfactory lot of hopeless endeavor, where the very *genius loci* was against him.

Therefore, early in October, 1816, when Abraham was nearly eight years old, and had been in school but a brief period, the family removed to Indiana, and settled in Spencer County, in the southern part of the State, near the Ohio River, about midway between Louisville and Evansville.

The farm and homestead which Thomas Lincoln sold could not have been very valuable; for the equivalent received was ten barrels of whiskey, valued at two hundred and eighty dollars, and twenty dollars in money. Mr. Lincoln was a temperate man, and consented to this arrangement, not from any love of the "fire-water," but because it was a customary transaction, and, in those days, regarded as perfectly proper.

The following description of the exodus from Kentucky presents such a graphic idea of the early days of President Lincoln, that it is quoted *verbatim*. The author is anonymous; but it is believed to be correct in every particular: —

"The homestead was within a mile or two of the Rolling Fork River; and, as soon as the sale was effected, Mr. Lincoln, with such slight assistance as little Abe could give him, hewed out a flat-boat, and, launching it, filled it with his household articles and tools and the barrels of whiskey, and bidding adieu to his son, who stood upon the bank, pushed off, and was soon floating down the stream, on his way to Indiana to select a new home. His journey down the Rolling Fork and into the Ohio River was successfully accomplished; but, soon afterwards, his boat was unfortunately upset, and its cargo thrown into the water. Some men standing on the bank witnessed the accident, and saved the boat and its owner; but all the contents of the craft were lost, except a few carpenter's tools, axes, three barrels of whiskey, and some other articles. He again started, and proceeded to a well-known ferry on the river, from whence he was guided into the interior by a resident of the section of country in which he had landed, and to whom he had given his boat in payment for his services. After several days of difficult travelling, much of the time employed in cutting a road through the forest wide enough for a team, eighteen miles were accomplished, and Spencer County, Ind., was reached. The site for his new home having been determined upon, Mr. Lincoln left his goods under the care of a person who lived a few miles distant, and, returning to Kentucky on foot, made preparations to remove his family. In a few days, the party bade farewell to their old home and slavery; Mrs. Lincoln and her daughter riding one horse, Abe another, and the father a third. After a seven-days' journey through an uninhabited country, their resting-place at night being a blanket spread upon the ground, they arrived at the spot selected for their future residence; and no unnecessary delays were permitted to interfere with the immediate and successful clearing of a site for a cabin. An axe was placed in Abe's hands; and, with the additional assistance of a neighbor, in two or three days Mr. Lincoln had a neat house of about eighteen feet square, the logs composing which being fastened together in the usual manner by notches, and the cracks between them filled with mud. It had only one room; but some slabs laid across logs overhead gave additional accommodations, which were obtained by climbing a rough ladder in one corner. A bed, table, and four stools, were then made by the two settlers, father and son; and the building was ready for occupancy. The loft was Abe's bed-room; and there, night after night, for many years, he who now occupies the most exalted position in the gift of the American people, and who dwells in the White House at Washington, surrounded by all the comforts that wealth and power can give, slumbered, with one coarse blanket for his mattress, and another for his covering.

LINCOLN'S EARLY HOME IN KENTUCKY.

"Although busy during the ensuing winter with his axe, he did not neglect his reading and spelling, and also practised frequently with a rifle; the first evidence of his skill as a marksman being manifested, much to the delight of his parents, in the killing of a wild turkey, which had approached too near the cabin. The knowledge of the use of the rifle was indispensable in the border settlements at that time, as the greater portion of the food required for the settlers was procured by it; and the family which had not among its male members one or more who could discharge it with accuracy was very apt to suffer from a scarcity of comestibles."

When Abe went to Mr. Hazel's school in Kentucky he took with him a copy of Dillworth's Spelling-book, one of the three books which composed the whole of the family library. The Bible and Catechism were the other two. Diligently conned, and even well-studied, his scanty early library did much to form the character of the child and the man. The spelling-book was the key to unlock for him all the treasures of knowledge he afterward made his own. From Æsop's lesson-fraught fables, soon after presented to him, he gained the aptness of illustration which has made "the President's last anecdote" a byword; and from the best of books and Catechism he gathered those ripe sheaves of wisdom which fitted him for his place in life and in history.

His mother — noble and blessed woman — was his inspiration. She was determined that her son should at least learn to read his Bible; and, before God called her to dwell with the angels, she had the satisfaction of seeing him read the volume which he never afterward neglected. Abraham's mother might have said, as did Mary the mother of Jesus, "From henceforth all generations shall call me blessed;" and while this nation shall revere the name and memory of the mother of George Washington, side by side with hers will it write the name of the mother of Abraham Lincoln. The parallel between Washington and Lincoln does not linger here. It pauses not till the bells toll a requiem, and a nation once more weeps over its beloved dead. True, there were apparent points of difference, but only such as, under Providence, were needed to fit each for their separate duties and destinies as leaders of the American people in their two great wars, — one for national independence, the other for national unity.

Washington was of a family renowned in English

heraldry. Lincoln could trace an honorable descent from Quaker stock in Pennslyvania.

"Washington was the natural representative of national independence. He might also have represented national unity, had this principle been challenged to bloody battle during his life; for nothing was nearer his heart than the consolidation of our Union, which, in his letter to Congress transmitting the Constitution, he declared to be the greatest interest of every true American. . . . But another person was needed, of different birth and simpler life, to represent the ideas which were now assailed." *

There were not a few *contrasts* — in origin, in early life, in condition and opportunities — between Washington and Lincoln, but the parallels are more numerous; and Washington himself had a mighty influence on the boy Lincoln through the record of his life, which Abraham read while yet a dweller in the rude log-cabin on the outskirts of civilization. One biographer † of Lincoln says, "The hatchet story of Washington, which has done more to make boys truthful than a hundred solemn exhortations, made a strong impression upon Abraham, and was one of those unseen, gentle influences which helped to form his character for integrity and honesty. Its effect may be traced in the following story, which bids fair to become as never-failing an accompaniment to a Life of Lincoln as the hatchet case to that of Washington: —

"Mr. Crawford had lent him a copy of Ramsay's 'Life of Washington.' During a severe storm, Abraham improved his leisure by reading this book. One night he laid it down carefully, as he thought, and the next morn-

* "Eulogy on Abraham Lincoln," by Hon. Charles Sumner.
† Henry J. Raymond.

ing he found it soaked through. The wind had changed, the storm had beaten in through a crack in the logs, and the appearance of the book was ruined. How could he face the owner under such circumstances? He had no money to offer as a return; but he took the book, went directly to Mr. Crawford, showed him the irreparable injury, and frankly and honestly offered to work for him until he should be satisfied. Mr. Crawford accepted the offer, and gave Abraham the book for his own in return for three days' steady labor in 'pulling fodder.' His manliness and straight-forwardness won the esteem of the Crawfords, and indeed of all the neighborhood."

Rev. William M. Thayer states, probably on the authority of those who knew Abraham Lincoln in early life, that, "during the long winter evenings of that first winter in Indiana, he read by the light of the fire only; for they could not afford the luxury of any other light in their cabin. This was true, very generally, of the pioneer families: they had no more than was absolutely necessary to supply their wants. They could exist without lamp-oil or candles, and so most of them did without either. They could afford the largest fire possible, since wood was so plenty that they studied to get rid of it. Hence the light of the fire was almost equal to a good chandelier. Large logs and branches of wood were piled together in the fireplace, and its mammoth blaze lighted up every nook and corner of the dwelling. Hence lamps were scarcely needed." *

Not long after the removal of the family to Indiana, the mother of Lincoln died. This was a sad loss to the whole of the little circle, especially to the children. Abraham had one sister who lived to womanhood, was

* "The Pioneer Boy," p. 102.

married, and died shortly after, leaving no children. His only brother died in infancy. Mrs. Lincoln, as has been intimated, was one of the most devoted of mothers, sparing no pains to insure the welfare of her beloved children. Abraham was always a dutiful son, and her counsel and example were not lost on him, but, as good seed sown on good ground, her instructions sprang forth into a life of good order and usefulness. The bereaved boy was almost inconsolable at her loss. No minister was near to pray with the survivors as they laid down the dear head of the wife and mother for the last, long sleep amid the shadows of the forest. Sympathizing neighbors gathered around; but the want of a minister to conduct the usual solemn rites of Christian burial was deeply felt. Some months afterward, Abraham had an opportunity of learning to write, which with characteristic energy and industry he faithfully improved. "After a few weeks of practice under the eye of his instructor, and also out of doors with a piece of chalk or charred stick, he was able to write his name, and in less than twelve months could and did write a letter."

One of the first letters he wrote was to an old friend of his mother, a travelling preacher, whom he desired to come and preach her funeral sermon. Parson Elkins did not receive the letter for some three months; but then he hastened to Indiana, and the neighbors again assembled — a year after her death — to pay a last tribute of respect to one universally beloved. Abraham's services as a letter-writer were thus known, and he soon found himself busied in writing letters for his neighbors.

President Lincoln never forgot his mother. It was very long before the loneliness and desolation of that sad bereavement passed away. Her lessons of divinest wisdom he kept stored in his heart, and all her hallowed influence was eternally sealed upon his soul by her departure from earth. Who shall say that it was not deepened and intensified by that very change which gave her henceforth more intimate communion with spirits, and possibly with the spirit of her son ? Her grave, to which hallowed spot the bereaved son was wont frequently to repair, and muse upon his great loss and her eternal gain, is still embowered amid the majestic forest-trees of that region. No tombstone yet denotes the sacred spot; and the place where the remains lie buried is an unfrequented locality, or nearly so. President Lincoln wrote a letter, shortly before his death, expressing his intention to visit the grave during the approaching summer, and cause a suitable monument to be erected; and in that letter, which was to an old friend, he expressed regret that care and business had so long hindered him from performing this duty.

He will never perform it. Instead of going to her grave, he has gone to her; and blissful beyond human computation must have been, ere this, the meeting of such a mother with such a son. Yet that humble grave should not be neglected. A nation owes it to the memory of a President martyred in its holy cause that his mother's tomb should be honorably distinguished.

During the next year after Mrs. Lincoln's death, Abraham's father married again, and secured in Mrs. Sally Johnston of Elizabethtown, Kentucky, a worthy stepmother for his children. She had three children, and seemed to have been one who could say with Mrs. Howe, —

> "Then spoke the angel of mothers
> To me in gentle tone,
> 'Be kind to the children of others,
> And thus deserve thine own.'"

Between her and the son to whom she became a true

friend as well as a step-mother sprang up a devoted attachment; and she ever acted as if she said to him in tender tones of ardent sympathy, using the words of Mrs. Welby, —

> " Child of the lost, the buried, and the sainted,
> I call thee mine,
> Till fairer still, with tears and sin untainted,
> Her home be thine."

Step-mothers are not all heartless, and those who, like the writer of these pages, have known the devoted care and tender love of a *good step-mother*, do not like to hear them as a class condemned. This second mother of our late President still survives to remember his nobleness of soul, and to mourn his martyrdom. She resides at Goose Nest, Coles County, eight miles south of Charlestown, Illinois.

A few years after the death of his mother, a Mr. Crawford, one of the settlers, opened a school in his own cabin; and thither Abraham regularly repaired to add a knowledge of arithmetic to his reading and writing. His appearance was in keeping with his humble home. He was arrayed in buckskin clothes, with a raccoon-skin cap, and carried an *old* arithmetic, which had been industriously sought for his benefit. "His progress was rapid, and his perseverance and faithfulness won the interest and esteem of his teacher." His love of books continued, and he read all that he could obtain far and near. With the immortal dreamer of Bedford jail, he traced the pathway of the Christian pilgrim from the City of Destruction to his Celestial Home beyond the river; and no doubt he felt that he, too, would gladly follow such a path, sure as he was that his own dear mother would be one of the shining ones to greet him on the heavenly shore. He pored over such books as the "Lives of Clay and Washington," till the fires of a noble emulation and true patriotism glowed in his heart; and he thus daily grew more and more to be of the very spirit of which heroic leaders and wise counsellors are made. God was fitting him, even in his childhood and his youth, for the very work which was before him. Bishop Simpson expressed this idea in his funeral sermon at Springfield, Illinois, on the 4th of May, 1865. He said, "Mr. Lincoln was no ordinary man. I believe the conviction has been growing on the nation's mind, as it certainly has been on my own, especially in the last years of his administration, that by the hand of God he was especially singled out to guide our Government in these troublesome times; and it seems to me that the hand of God may be traced in many of the events connected with his history. First, then, I recognize this in the physical education which he received, and which prepared him for enduring herculean labors. In the toils of his boyhood, and the labors of his manhood, God was giving him an iron frame. Next to this was his identification with the heart of this great people, understanding their feelings because he was one of them, and connected with them in their movements and life. His education was simple. A few months spent in the schoolhouse gave him the elements of education. He read few books, but mastered all he read. 'Pilgrim's Progress,' 'Æsop's Fables,' and the 'Life of Washington,' were his favorites. In these we recognize the works which gave the bias to his character, and which partly moulded his style. His early life, with its varied struggles, joined him indissolubly to the working masses; and no elevation in society diminished his respect for the sons of toil. He knew what it was to fell the tall trees of the forest, and to stem the current of the broad Mississippi.

His home was in the growing West, the heart of the Republic; and, invigorated by the wind which swept over its prairies, he learned lessons of self-reliance which sustained him in seasons of adversity."

Bishop Simpson's allusion to Abraham's efforts on the broad bosom of the "Father of Waters" was founded, doubtless, on the fact, that, when about nineteen years of age, Abraham accompanied the son of the owner of a flatboat, who intrusted a valuable cargo to their care, to the city of New Orleans. He was hired at the rate of

FLATBOAT.

ten dollars a month, and the twain composed the only crew. With only one companion, it was rather a dangerous journey. "At night they tied up alongside of the bank, and rested upon the hard deck, with a blanket for a covering; and during the hours of light, whether their lonely trip was cheered by a bright sun, or made disagreeable in the extreme by violent storms, their craft floated down the stream, its helmsmen never for a moment losing their spirits, or regretting their acceptance of the positions they occupied. Nothing occurred to mar the success of the trip, nor the excitement naturally incident to a flatboat expedition of some eighteen hundred miles, save a midnight attack by a party of negroes, who, after a severe conflict, were compelled to flee."

In the spring of 1830, the Lincoln family again sought a new home. Their journey, in a region where roads were rough and railroads unknown, was made in fifteen days. They carried their goods in large wagons drawn by oxen, and Abraham himself drove one of the teams. They halted on the north side of the Sangamon River, at a place about ten miles west of Decatur, Illinois. While crossing the bottom lands of the Kaskaskia River on their way, the men of the party were obliged to wade through water several feet deep. So the journey was not accomplished without some hinderances. On their arrival a log-cabin was to be built, ground broken for corn, and a rail-fence to be made around the farm, in all of which Abraham labored faithfully.* Those rails have been im-

LINCOLN'S FIRST HOUSE IN ILLINOIS.

* In this work the Lincolns were assisted by a relative of Abraham's mother, named John Hanks. While this volume was in preparation, Mr. Hanks was in Boston exhibiting this identical log-cabin, together with other relics

mortalized by orators and poets, and will henceforth be mentioned by historians. Sumner says, "These rails have become classical in our history, and the name of 'rail-splitter' has been more than the degree of a college. Not that the splitter of rails is especially meritorious, but because the people are proud to trace aspiring talent to humble beginnings, and because they found in this tribute a new opportunity of vindicating the dignity of free labor, and of repelling the insolent pretensions of slavery." The newspaper report of the first public mention of Abraham Lincoln as a rail-splitter is as follows: "During the sitting of the Republican State Convention at Decatur, a banner attached to two of these rails, and bearing an appropriate inscription, was brought into the assemblage, and formally presented to that body, amid a scene of unparalleled enthusiasm. After that, they were in demand in every State in the Union in which free labor is honored, where they were borne in processions of the people, and hailed by hundreds of thousands of freemen as a symbol of triumph, and as a glorious vindication of freedom and of the rights and dignity of free labor. These, however, were far from being the first or only rails made by Lincoln. He was a practised hand at the business. Mr. Lincoln has now a cane made from one of the rails split by his own hands in boyhood."

of Lincoln's early days of poverty and obscurity. He is an honest-looking gentleman, with a silvery beard, about seven years older than Mr. Lincoln, but much more venerable in appearance. He can neither read nor write. He says that his cousin Dennis F. Hanks taught "little Abe" his letters. The log-cabin above mentioned has no windows; but a half sheet of paper oiled, placed in a sort of wooden shutter, admitted a little light when the shutter was closed. It is said to be truly a Union cabin, having in it sticks of oak, hickory, hackberry, red elm, walnut, basswood, honey, locust, and sassafras, but, it is believed, not a stick of pine. The dimensions are eighteen feet by sixteen; and it is nine logs, or about eight feet, high. It has a peaked roof, the highest part of which is about five feet from the level of its eaves. It was begun March 30, 1830; and four days were spent in building it.

Thus in the foregoing pages have been depicted the events and influences of Abraham Lincoln's life during his early days. In the eloquent language of his eulogist in the "Athens of America," on the day set apart for commemorative services all over the land, this chapter may be fittingly closed: —

"His youth was now spent, and at the age of twenty-one he left his father's house to begin the world for himself. A small bundle, a laughing face, and an honest heart, — these were his visible possessions, together with that unconscious character and intelligence which his country afterward learned to prize. In the long history of 'worth depressed,' there is no instance of such a contrast between the depression and the triumph, unless, perhaps, his successor as President may share with him this distinction. No academy, no university, no alma mater of science or learning, had nourished him. No government had taken him by the hand, and given to him the gift of opportunity. No inheritance of land or money had fallen to him. No friend stood by his side. He was alone in poverty; and yet not all alone. There was God above, who watches all, and does not desert the lowly. Simple in life and manners, and knowing nothing of form or ceremony, with a village schoolmaster for six months as his only teacher, he had grown up in companionship with the people, with nature, with trees, with the fruitful corn, and with the stars. While yet a child, his father had borne him away from a soil wasted by slavery; and he was now the citizen of a free State, where free labor had been placed under the safeguard of irreversible compact and fundamental law. And thus closed the youth of the future President, happy at least that he could go forth under the day-star of Liberty."

CHAPTER II.

CULTURE.

"The more our spirits are enlarged on earth,
The deeper draught will they receive of heaven."

"The righteous shall flourish like the palm-tree; he shall grow like a cedar in Lebanon." — PSALM xcii. 12.

THE celebrated German poet Goethe once made this instructive declaration, in a conversation with his friend Eckerman: "Each *bon-mot* has cost me a purse of gold: half a million of my own money, the fortune I inherited, my salary, and the large income I have derived from my writings for fifty years back, have been expended to instruct me in what I know." Men are apt to overlook the stupendous price at which they have every thing; and the culture which has only been secured through a civilization which has cost suffering and toil and thought, and even heroism and martyrdom, is still deemed to have been obtained without much expenditure, when, in fact, it was priceless; so much so, that to ask its amount is almost like asking, with the Lord Jesus, "What shall it profit a man if he gain the whole world and lose his own soul? or what shall a man give in exchange for his soul?"

We think of that log-cabin in the woods, of the inelegant surroundings of the future President, and say, "Such a man was not cultured, and it cost nothing to train him for duty and destiny." But it did cost much: not, it may be, of money, though more of that than a superficial observer might suppose; but labor and influence and prayers, and the silent but powerful ministrations of Nature and Nature's God with his angelic messengers, who are declared to be "ministering spirits, sent forth to minister for them who shall be heirs of salvation."

Abraham Lincoln was not a man of science, or a literary man, as men often use those terms. He would not be classed with Humboldt or Newton, nor with Scott or Irving; but he was nevertheless a man of culture. *Labor* made him such; his own earnest efforts to gain learning, his parents' efforts that he should obtain at least the rudiments of an education, and enter, at all events, the porch of the temple of wisdom, and the labor of instructors who must have been encouraged by the earnest attention and patient industry of the boy for whom God had in store a high place and a noble work. *Influence* — the influence of mighty rulers in the realm of mind, mighty though few — was brought to bear upon his nascent spirit for its growth and culture. Plutarch and Æsop, Washington, and Franklin, and Clay, lived for Abraham Lincoln, as well as for others whom they have influenced in the paths of honor and virtue. And the tinker of Bedford, whose immortal allegory wreathes its author's head with the unfading laurels, — he, too, had no mean part in the culture of a man who has proved himself often a Great-Heart, but never a Worldly-wise-Man. And, above all, the historians and prophets of ancient times, the Hebrew bards whose harps will never cease to echo through the ages, the apostolic teachers of the dawning Christian era, and especially He who "spake as never man spake," — all had their mighty and far-reaching influence on the mind of the boy, who, like young Timothy, studied the Holy Scriptures, and early accepted them as a "lamp to his feet and a light to his path."

Prayers, too, had something to do with his culture.

There may be those who scoff at prayer, who scout the idea once expressed in rhythmical harmony, that—

"Prayer moves the hand which moves the world;"

but as there are forces in Nature whose origin and influence we cannot fully explain, while yet we are compelled to acknowledge their existence; so, though we may not comprehend how prayer accomplishes its divinely appointed ends, yet it is none the less true that *prayer is a power in the universe.* Other things being equal, he that has most power in prayer is surest of success; for in prayer he takes hold of the arm of God, joins to his weakness the infinite strength, and finds himself possessed of the true Archimedean lever.

Abraham Lincoln's mother was a praying woman. "She who would rather her son would 'learn to read his Bible than own a farm' was a true, model mother; and when in his early childhood a green mound in the wilderness showed that she had finished her course, and gained her reward, well might that boy Lincoln visit that holy place, and weep for very bitterness of soul."* The prayers of such a woman must have been answered in the dew of grace that early fell upon the soul of her motherless boy. There were other prayers, too, which undoubtedly had their unseen influence in the culture of Abraham Lincoln. Far away in the rice-swamps and cotton-plantations of the South, a long-oppressed race were crying for deliverance. Worse task-masters than those of Egypt were crushing out the very manhood and womanhood of the slavery-cursed people; and the despairing cry of agony went up to heaven, in the tears and groans and prayers of long, long years, for a de-

* Rev. A. Caldwell's Address.

liverer. God heard those prayers; and slowly to our eyes and to their waiting hearts, but more surely for the fulfilment of his own grand purposes of love and mercy, he prepared the man who should grasp the keys of destiny with a firm hand but a tender heart, and unlock the doors of the prison-house. And so prayer cultured Abraham Lincoln.

But how describe the culture which that great soul received from Nature with her myriad forms of beauty, and from God and the angels? The receptive mind, consciously or unconsciously (and more often the latter), is powerfully impressed with the wonders of the outward world; and Abraham Lincoln was one of those who could not witness that awakening of the spring-time, which Longfellow calls "the great annual miracle of Nature," without receiving lasting and salutary impressions. So, too, the "soft summer-time," autumn with its golden glory, and the winter with its crystals of geometric beauty covering the earth with a snowy carpet, — all taught him divinest lessons. There was no Vatican, nor British Museum, nor Astor Library, with their myriad volumes, to aid in his intellectual culture; but he early learned to find —

"Tongues in the trees, books in the running brooks,
Sermons in stones, and good in every thing;"

and his young soul grew more and more.

Angels from the world of light hovered around his pathway, as long ago around his Lord, and as they encamp around all God's dear children. The dream of Doddridge, which showed him an angel-guardian in many a scene of danger through which he had passed, was but a truthful expression of the fact that the "cloud of witnesses" ever around the immortal but earth-veiled spirit of the child of God are fulfilling grand purposes of blessing to the soul they guard.

Above all, Abraham Lincoln was taught of God. The "still small voice" was not unheard by him from early infancy. His own prayers mingled with those already mentioned, and the Great Spirit heard and answered. The divine utterance in his own soul was not unheeded; and day by day listening to it, and heeding its requirements, he not only "grew in wisdom and in stature," but, like the Holy Child, he also "grew in favor with God and man."

"The man who is complete in that for which the world wants him," as Abraham Lincoln was, "seems not only to be suited for his work, but to have had all circumstances suited to him. He is born in the right age of history. The proper spot of earth waits for him and receives him. The household into which he enters appears best for him amidst all the households of humanity. So perhaps it might not be judged in many a case if we saw the man in the first stages of his nurture; but so we find it when we can see his life in its issues. A similar adaptation may be noticed in any remarkable man's tastes, trials, and pursuits; in all, indeed, that subserves his training and his experience."* Abraham Lincoln became just such a remarkable man, after a youth spent in receiving just the culture of heart and mind needed for his place in the world.

The early days of Lincoln, spent in the obscurity of his forest home, have already been traced. His removal to Illinois brought him to new scenes, and under new influences. He was now to be cultured by society in a greater degree than ever before.

* "Illustrations of Genius," by Rev. Henry Giles.

Having passed his twenty-first birthday, he began in 1831 to labor for himself. He aided to build a flatboat, and then went in it to New Orleans, and so satisfactorily cared for boat and cargo, that his employer took him into his store at New Salem, twenty miles below Springfield. Here for a twelvemonth he became more familiar with arithmetic; and here he so dealt with his customers, and so conducted himself in all the relations of life, that he began to be known as "Honest Abe," — an honorable title which will never be taken away; for he never forfeited it.

Athletic and active, young Lincoln could not fail to engage in the usual out-door sports of young men in that place, and was usually the acknowledged judge of the games, whose integrity or good judgment was unquestionable.

It cannot be said that the culture of Abraham Lincoln was that which would make him shine in polite society. His uncouth, awkward form and homely visage, his unpolished dress and address, were to be expected from his pioneer life; but his soul was robed in beauty which the angels could discern, and which all high souls, to whom he was known on earth, sooner or later perceived. His culture was such as many a man of humble birth and lowly home may share, and it brought him into sympathy with the people over whom he was to be placed, and clothed him with true humility when he stood on the pinnacle of power and fame. It was a culture which produced simplicity, that child-like charm which won all appreciative hearts to the Martyr-President. "Simplicity adapts itself artlessly to others, because it is full of charity, and therefore desires to make others happy. Its words are the overflow of genial thought and kindly affection; and all hearts that hold aught in common with it open and expand before its influences, as plants start at the touch of spring. . . . There is no affectation, no straining for effect, in simplicity. All is natural and genuine with it. Its wit is never forced, its wisdom is never stilted; nor is either ever dragged in for mere display." *

This rare simplicity was a special result of the culture which President Lincoln received; and, while the hand of God is plainly to be observed in all his history, nowhere is it more prominently seen than in the circumstances and influences which helped to make Lincoln what he was,—a man whose culture was not scientific or literary mainly, but just such as would make a man of the people fit to govern the people in righteousness and love.

* "Elements of Character," by Mrs. Mary G. Ware.

CHAPTER III.

PREPARATION FOR HIS WORK.

"Walk
Boldly and wisely in that light thou hast:
There is a hand above will help thee on."
BAILEY'S *Festus.*

"Stand therefore, having your loins girt about with truth, and having on the breastplate of righteousness, and your feet shod with the preparation of the gospel of peace; above all, taking the shield of faith, wherewith ye shall be able to quench all the fiery darts of the wicked. And take the helmet of salvation, and the sword of the Spirit, which is the word of God." — ST. PAUL (Eph. vi. 14-17).

VEIL the truth as we may, if indisposed to see it, yet, nevertheless, there will come shining through the mighty fact that God had a work for Abraham Lincoln to perform, and that he prepared him for it, not by giving him wealthy friends, inherited honors, splendid position, but by permitting him to be inured to toil and hardship and bereavement, and thus to

"Know how sublime a thing it is
To suffer and be strong."

Day by day, amid the peculiar circumstances of his early days and opening manhood, was he putting on the armor which should be needed in the hours of stern conflict that were approaching. Well has one * said, "Lap of luxury and home of ease send not forth the arms that move the world. He who is driven aloft by the force of circumstances becomes the noblest soul and the mighti-

* Rev. Augustine Caldwell.

est power. Call we a humble home, a scanty board, and threadbare coat, but a blight or curse? Ah!

> 'God, in cursing,
> Gives us better gifts than men in blessing;'

and those humble ones who have struggled upward with nothing but a stern will and a consciousness of right to uphold them have proved the world's richest friends."

The Lord Jesus teaches, in his pertinent question concerning the falling sparrow and the numbered hairs, that God exercises a constant watchfulness over all men, and continually guides them in the affairs of life. The history of our late President's career, and of the times in which he lived, everywhere shows the guiding hand of a divine providence.

"Many are willing to acknowledge a general providence, who do not believe in a universal or particular one. But there cannot be a general providence without a particular one. That would be utterly impossible; for all generals are made up of particulars. Could a man cultivate a farm in general, without ploughing any particular field, or casting into the earth any particular seeds? Could a watchmaker make watches in general, without making any particular wheels and springs, and giving to every wheel its special form and size and place, finishing the minutest parts in the nicest manner? Could a merchant sell things in general, and nothing in particular, having no particular store, or particular goods, or special price? Or if we look at the material creation, where we can see the divine method of working, does the Lord make a tree in general, without any particular branches, twigs, leaves, bark, fibre, and cells? No: on the contrary, the whole tree is built up by the action of the pores and cells in their least parts. This is the universal method of the divine operations. . . . It is impossible that there can be a general providence without a special one. If there is a general providence, it is the result of a universal or particular one."*

The great work of Abraham Lincoln was to guide the American Ship of State during the storm of rebellion, and, as an indissoluble duty, to emancipate the oppressed millions in our land, whose unrighteous bondage made our glorious banner too long a "flaunting lie," and our "Independent days" ostentatious cheats. We have seen how his childhood and early manhood were the precursors of a useful maturity; and still may we trace the guiding hand of God in his further steps, preparing him for the Presidency of the United States, and to be Commander-in-Chief of the Union Army.

Before the death of his mother, the future director of the greatest army the world ever saw was taught the use of fire-arms; and it is worthy of note that the mother of Lincoln — brave pioneer woman that she was! — herself loaded the rifle with which he then shot his first game, — a large wild turkey. He became very expert in the use of the rifle; and, as has been already intimated, was able thus to add to the family larder, and also to procure furs, which were then in great demand.

One of his biographers says, "There is no doubt that the culture he received by the use of the rifle had its influence in developing his physical energies, as he was ever distinguished for his strength and powers of endurance; and that it indirectly served to inspire his heart with courage, promptness, and decision, for which his whole life has been eminent."†

The same biographer relates a circumstance which happened during the time when Abraham attended Mr.

* Rev. Chauncy Giles. † "Pioneer Boy," p. 11.

Crawford's school, that illustrates the growing capacity of the lad, and foreshadows his future labors as a public speaker. The scholars were talking, one Monday morning before the hour for school to commence, about the sermon to which they had listened the day before. Abraham declared himself able to repeat a large part of the sermon; and, when the boys doubted it, he proved his retentive memory, close attention, and speech-making powers, by mounting a stump and rehearsing the sermon. The young orator was overheard by his teacher, and won his admiration and applause as well as that of his fellow-pupils. Little did any of them think how he would address large audiences in the future just unfolding before him, swaying their minds and influencing their hearts by a forcible and earnest presentation of high truths intimately connected with the safety and happiness of the nation.

He, of whom one of his early associates says, "We seldom went hunting together; Abe was not a noted hunter, as the time spent by other boys in such amusements was improved by him in the perusal of some good book," did not fail to grow in knowledge ever after he left his father's roof, and sought to carve his own way to fame and fortune, wholly ignorant of the lofty niche assigned him in the temple of renown.

Mr. Lincoln, for so he should be called since he was twenty-one and had an indisputable right to wear the *toga virilis*, sought employment among those who needed a strong arm, and exemplified in his own efforts the sensible words which he uttered thirty years later in reference to hired labor: —

"My understanding of the hired laborer is this: A young man finds himself of an age to be dismissed from parental control; he has for his capital nothing save two strong hands that God has given him, a heart willing to labor, and a freedom to choose the mode of his work, and the manner of his employer; he has no soil nor shop, and he avails himself of the opportunity of hiring himself to some man who has capital to pay him a fair day's wages for a fair day's work. He is benefited by availing himself of that privilege; he works industriously, he behaves soberly, and the result of a year or two's labor is a surplus of capital. Now he buys land on his own hook; he settles, marries, begets sons and daughters; and, in course of time, he, too, has enough capital to hire some new beginner."

This homely and characteristic speech was truthful, like the man who uttered it when on the eve of nomination to the highest office in the gift of the nation; and at that same time he expressed his opinion in regard to free labor, in the same straightforward, though rather inelegant manner. His words may as well be quoted here. They were these: "Our Government was not established that one man might do with himself as he pleases, and with another man too. . . . I say, that, whereas God Almighty has given every man one mouth to be fed, and one pair of hands adapted to furnish food for that mouth, if any thing can be proved to be the will of Heaven, it is proved by this fact, that that mouth is to be fed by those hands, without being interfered with by any other man, who has also his mouth to feed and his hands to labor with. I hold, if the Almighty had ever made a set of men that should do all the eating and none of the work, he would have made them with mouths only, and no hands; and if he had ever made another class that he had intended should do all the work, and none of the eating, he would have made them without mouths, and with all hands."

As a hired laborer, young Lincoln spent the summer and fall with a Mr. Armstrong, who observed his studious habits, and proposed to his wife to keep the youthful student through the winter. He insisted on laboring for Mr. Armstrong enough to pay his board, and spent the rest of his time in study.

Early the next spring, as before stated, he assisted in building a boat at Sangamon, and then made a trip to New Orleans, which was so successful, that his employer, gratified with the industry and tact young Lincoln exhibited, engaged him to take charge of his mill and store in the village of New Salem. Thus Mr. Lincoln, having already been prepared to sympathize with the mechanic, came to have a near relation also to the merchant, that he could understand in after-life the trials and preplexities of that class among the men he was called to govern.

The young man who spent his leisure moments, amid the distractions of mercantile life, in studying grammar and arithmetic, may well be supposed to feel an interest in public events transpiring in his native land.

Early in the year 1832 the Black-Hawk War commenced, and the Governor of Illinois called for volunteer troops. Young Lincoln, with patriotic ardor, was the first to place his name on the roll at the recruiting-office in New Salem. A company was soon raised there; and such was the confidence of his fellow-townsmen and comrades-in-arms, that they unanimously chose him to be their captain,—an office which he reluctantly accepted, having a modest doubt of his own ability to serve in that capacity.

"The New-Salem company went into camp at Beardstown, from whence, in a few days, they marched to the expected scene of conflict. When the thirty days of their enlistment had expired, however, they had not seen the enemy. They were disbanded at Ottawa, and most of the volunteers returned; but, a new levy being called for, Abraham re-enlisted as a private. Another thirty days expired, and the war was not over. His regiment was disbanded, and again, the third time, he volunteered. He was determined to serve his country as long as the war lasted. Before the third term of his enlistment had expired, the battle of Bad Axe was fought, which put an end to the war.

"He returned home. 'Having lost his horse, near where the town of Janesville, Wisconsin, now stands, he went down Rock River to Dixon in a canoe; thence he crossed the country on foot to Peoria, where he again took canoe to a point on the Illinois River, within forty miles of home. The latter distance he accomplished on foot.'

"One who served under him in the New-Salem company writes, that he was a universal favorite in the army; that he was an efficient, faithful officer, watchful of his men, and prompt in the discharge of duty; and that his courage and patriotism shrank from no dangers or hardships." *

Thus by personal participation in military duties the future Commander-in-Chief was preparing for his coming responsibilities; and this preparation was such as to make him truly sympathize with privates as well as officers, and to be just to both.

He returned to New Salem and to business when no longer needed as a soldier. The author of the "Lincoln Memorial" says, in speaking of Mr. Lincoln as a clerk and manager, "He soon made his mark: an attempt of a gang of the bullies of the place to give him a beating resulted in the defeat of their champion by the tall sinewy stranger, who at once became a favorite with

* "The Pioneer Boy," p. 252.

those who gauged men by their physical endurance and courage; while his affable manners, his unfailing cheerfulness, his ready wit, and his stories, made him a favorite with all. A store was soon his own; but he was too honest and too kind-hearted to drive sharp bargains, and soon found himself in difficulties which it required years of subsequent struggle to clear away, but which he allowed to stand no longer than till he had ability to discharge them. Honest Abraham Lincoln knew no bankrupt's discharge, but a receipt in full on payment in full."

Another noticeable fact in Mr. Lincoln's history is thus mentioned by the same writer: "The office of postmaster of New Salem, a petty office indeed, was his first public position, and one which gave him intense pleasure from the opportunity of reading it afforded him; and it is not a little remarkable that he began life, we may say, by serving the General Government in a civil, and soon after in a military capacity."

The writer of the "Lincoln Memorial" thinks that the fact of Lincoln's captaincy was significant, and almost symbolical. "This early choice," he says, "of one who was at most a clerk and hand in a country store, shows how clearly his fellow-citizens had recognized him as one born to be a ruler of men. At the next election for members of the legislature, he was taken up as the candidate of his district, and so completely united the votes of all parties in his precinct, that he received every vote but seven out of two hundred and eighty-four; and though he was defeated in the district at large, it was the only occasion in which he failed in such an election."

While acting as postmaster, Mr. Lincoln continued his studies, and improved his increased opportunities for extensive reading. He is said to have written out a synopsis of every book he read, and thus to have fixed the contents in his memory.

About this time, John Calhoun, afterwards President of the Lecompton Constitutional Convention, and prominent in the troubles in Kansas, came to New Salem. He soon formed the acquaintance of the best conversationist in the place, and advised him to learn surveying, — the work in which he himself was engaged. Mr. Lincoln did so, and soon obtained employment as a surveyor, thus unconsciously imitating him whose place as the head of a great nation he was afterwards to occupy. Little thought Washington or Lincoln, as they drove their stakes or stretched their chains over their neighbors' lands "for a consideration," that they should one day, so to speak, drive the stakes of their tent in the Capitol of the nation, and stretch the chain of their influence over the whole broad country. But God "putteth down one, and setteth up another;" and he upon whose brow God has ordained a crown should rest will surely wear it in the fulness of time, though he may have been born in a hovel or a manger.

Difficulties beset the path of the future President. He had not the never-empty purse of Fortunatus, nor the power of the Phrygian king to turn every thing he touched to gold; and therefore he often found himself embarrassed in financial matters; and at one time, it is said, even his instruments used in surveying were actually seized for debt.

"He still took an active part in politics; and in August, 1834, he was elected to the legislature by a large majority. In this new field he learned much. He was a persistent student, and had already, by close application, made up for much of the deficiency of his early education. He analyzed all he read, and gave up nothing till he had thoroughly mastered it. This gave him a correctness and precision of thought which never failed him. Naturally modest, he discharged his legislative duties without any of the parade or elation which makes some inexperienced members mere tools of the wily politician, or personally ridiculous. His clearness and eloquence struck the Hon. John T. Stuart, one of his fellow-members, and he urged the young member to study law. Acting on this advice, he set himself to Blackstone with ardor, his favorite retreat being a wooded knoll in New Salem, where, stretched under an oak, he would pore over the doctrines of common law, utterly unconscious of all passing around him, and impressing some, at least, of his neighbors with doubts of his entire sanity."

The author of the "Pioneer Boy" thus refers to this period of study: "He canvassed the whole subject in the beginning, and he resolved to spend no evenings in social entertainments. He saw that he must do it from sheer necessity, as he would be obliged to use up the night-hours much more economically than the laws of health would permit. And now he was inflexible. His purpose was fixed, and no allurements or promises of pleasure could make him swerve a hair's-breadth therefrom.

"Springfield was twenty-two miles from New Salem; and yet Lincoln walked there and back on the day proposed. He made a long day of it, and a wearisome one too. On the following evening, Greene called upon him to learn how he made it.

"'What!' he exclaimed, 'did you bring all those books home in your arms?' They were 'Blackstone's Commentaries,' in four volumes.

"'Yes, and read one of the volumes more than half of the way,' Lincoln replied. 'Come, now, just examine me on that first volume.' He had a faculty of perusing a volume when he was walking, and he often did it. He gained time thereby.

"'I don't see what you are made of, to endure so,' continued Greene. 'It would use me all up to carry such a load a quarter part of that distance.'

"'I am used to it, you know; and that makes the difference. But, come, just see what I know about the first part of that volume.' And he passed the first volume to him.

"'If you pass muster, you'll want I should admit you to the bar, I suppose,' responded Greene humorously. 'That I shall be glad to do.'

"So he proceeded to examine Lincoln on the first volume; and he found, to his surprise, that he was well posted on every part of it that he had read. By his close attention, and the ability to concentrate his thoughts, he readily made what he read his own.

"Thus Lincoln began and continued the study of law, alternating his time between surveying and study; going to Springfield for books as often as it was necessary, and often pursuing his reading of law far into the night. People were universally interested in his welfare, and all predicted that he would make his mark by and by.

"With such devotion did he employ his time in study and manual labor, denying himself of much that young men generally consider essential, that he might have said with Cicero, 'What others give to public shows and entertainments, to festivity, to amusements, nay, even to mental and bodily rest, I give to study and philosophy.' Even when he was engaged in the fields surveying, his thoughts were upon his books, so that much which he learned at night was fastened in his mind by day. He might have said again with Cicero, 'Even my leisure hours have their occupation.'"

In 1836 he obtained a law-license, and in April, 1837, he removed to Springfield, and became the law-partner of Mr. Stuart; and, when the latter went to Congress, he became a partner of Judge Logan. One touching incident of his law-practice, which paints in vivid colors the character of Lincoln as a man and his ability as a lawyer, is thus narrated in a Cleveland paper: "Some few years since, the eldest son of Mr. Lincoln's old friend, Armstrong, — the chief supporter of his widowed mother, the good old man having some time previously passed from earth, — was arrested on the charge of murder. A young man had been killed during a riotous *mêlée* in the night-time, at a camp-meeting, and one of his associates stated that the death-wound was inflicted by young Armstrong. A preliminary examination was gone into, at which the accuser testified so positively, that there seemed no doubt of the guilt of the prisoner, and therefore he was held for trial. As is too often the case, the bloody act caused an undue degree of excitement in the public mind. Every improper incident in the life of the prisoner, each act which bore the least semblance of rowdyism, each school-boy quarrel, was suddenly remembered and magnified, until they pictured him as a fiend of the most horrible hue. As these rumors spread abroad, they were received as gospel truth, and a feverish desire for vengeance seized upon the infatuated populace, whilst only prison-bars prevented a horrible death at the hands of a mob. The events were heralded in the county papers, painted in the highest colors, accompanied by rejoicing over the certainty of punishment being meted out to the guilty party. The prisoner, overwhelmed by the circumstances under which he found himself placed, fell into a melancholy condition bordering on despair; and the widowed mother, looking through her tears, saw no cause for hope from earthly aid.

At this juncture the widow received a letter from Mr. Lincoln, volunteering his services in an effort to save the youth from the impending stroke. Gladly was his aid accepted, although it seemed impossible for even his sagacity to prevail in such a desperate case; but the heart of the attorney was in his work, and he set about it with a will that knew no such word as fail. Feeling that the poisoned condition of the public mind was such as to preclude the possibility of impanelling an impartial jury in the court having jurisdiction, he procured a change of venue and a postponement of the trial. He then went studiously to work, unravelling the history of the case, and satisfied himself that his client was the victim of malice, and that the statements of the accuser were a tissue of falsehoods.

When the trial was called on, the prisoner, pale and emaciated, with hopelessness written on every feature, and accompanied by his half-hoping, half-despairing mother, — whose only hope was in a mother's belief of her son's innocence, in the justice of the God she worshipped, and in the noble counsel, who, without hope of fee or reward upon earth, had undertaken the cause, — took his seat in the prisoner's box, and with a stony firmness listened to the reading of the indictment. Lincoln sat quietly by, whilst the large auditory looked on him as though wondering what he could say in defence of one whose guilt they regarded as certain.

The examination of the witnesses for the State was begun, and a well-arranged mass of evidence, circumstantial and positive, was introduced, which seemed to impale the prisoner beyond the possibility of extrication. The counsel for the defence propounded but few questions, and those of a character which excited no uneasiness on the part of the prosecutor; merely, in most cases, requiring the main witnesses to be definite as to the time and place. When the evidence of the prosecution was ended, Lincoln introduced a few witnesses to remove some erroneous impressions in regard to the previous character of his client, who, though somewhat rowdyish, had never been known to commit a vicious act, and to show that a greater degree of ill-feeling existed between the accuser and the accused than the accused and the deceased.

The prosecutor felt that the case was a clear one, and his opening speech was brief and formal. Lincoln arose, while a deathly silence pervaded the vast audience, and in a clear and moderate tone began his argument. Slowly and carefully he reviewed the testimony; pointing out the hitherto unobserved discrepancies in the statements of the principal witness. That which had seemed plain and plausible he made to appear crooked as a serpent's path. The witness had stated that the affair took place at a certain hour in the evening, and that, by the aid of a brightly shining moon, he saw the prisoner inflict the death-blow with a slung-shot. Mr. Lincoln showed that at the hour referred to the moon had not yet appeared above the horizon, and consequently the whole tale was a fabrication.

An almost instantaneous change seemed to have been wrought in the minds of his auditors, and the verdict of "Not Guilty" was at the end of every tongue. But the advocate was not content with this intellectual achievement. His whole being had for months been bound up in this work of gratitude and mercy; and as the lava of the over-charged crater bursts from its imprisonment, so great thoughts and burning words leaped forth from the soul of the eloquent Lincoln. He drew a picture of the perjurer, so horrid and ghastly that the accuser could sit under it no longer, but reeled and staggered from the court-room, whilst the audience fancied they could see the brand upon his brow. Then, in words of thrilling pathos, Lincoln appealed to the jurors, as fathers of some who might become fatherless, and husbands of wives who might be widowed, to yield to no previous impressions, no ill-founded prejudice, but to do his client justice; and as he alluded to the debt of gratitude which he owed the boy's sire, tears were seen to fall from many eyes unused to weep.

It was near night when he concluded by saying, that, if justice was done, — as he believed it would be, — before the sun should set, it would shine upon his client a free man. The jury retired, and the court adjourned for the day. Half an hour had not elapsed, when, as the officers of the court and the volunteer attorney sat at the tea-table of their hotel, a messenger announced that the jury had returned to their seats. All repaired immediately to the court-house; and whilst the prisoner was coming from the jail, the court-room was filled to overflowing with citizens from the town. When the prisoner and his mother entered, silence reigned as completely as though the house were empty. The foreman of the jury, in answer to the usual inquiry from the court, delivered the verdict of "Not Guilty!" The widow dropped into the arms of her son, who lifted her up, and told her to look upon him as before, free and innocent. Then with the words, "Where is Mr. Lincoln?" he rushed across the room and grasped the hand of his deliverer, whilst his heart was too full for utterance. Lincoln turned his eyes towards the west, where the sun still lingered in view, and then, turning to the youth, said, "It is not yet sundown, and you are free!" I confess that my cheeks were not wholly unwet by tears, and I turned from the affecting scene. As I cast a glance behind, I saw Abraham Lincoln obeying the divine injunction by comforting the widowed and fatherless.

Three times was Mr. Lincoln, after this, elected to the Legislature, and there commenced his political acquaintance with Stephen A. Douglas. He then remained several years in private life, practising law with good success. In 1842, he married Miss Mary Todd, daughter of Hon. Robert Todd of Lexington, Kentucky. Their children have been four in number: "Robert, recently a captain on Gen. Grant's staff, born in 1843; a second son, born in 1846, and William, born in 1850, both of whom are dead; and Thaddeus, born in 1853, who stands beside his father in the last photograph taken of the President.

"It gives some idea of the prominence of Mr. Lincoln in Illinois, that, though elected to the Legislature only in 1834, he was a Whig candidate for presidential elector at every election from 1836 to 1852. An early and warm admirer of Henry Clay, he came forward, in 1844, and stumped the entire State of Illinois in his favor, and then crossed into Indiana, attracting attention by the homely force, humor, energy, and eloquence of his addresses. Thus thrown again into active politics, he was elected to Congress in 1846, from the Central District of Illinois, by a majority of fifteen hundred, being the only Whig member from the State. Called now into the great council of the nation, Mr. Lincoln took his seat among great men. In the Senate, Clay, Calhoun, Webster, Benton, still shaped the destinies and restrained the passions of men; and men of great ability stood forth in the lower House. Mr. Lincoln was opposed to the annexation of Texas and to the Mexican War. He voted many times—'about forty,' he once said—for the Wilmot Proviso; thus as early as 1847 showing himself the same friend of freedom in the Territories which he was afterwards when 'bleeding Kansas' received his sympathy. 'On other great questions which came before Congress, Mr. Lincoln, being a Whig, took the ground which was held by the great body of his party. He believed in the right of Congress to make appropriations for the improvement of rivers and harbors. He was in favor of giving the public lands, not to speculators, but to actual occupants and cultivators, at as low rates as possible; and he was in favor of a protective tariff, and of abolishing the franking privilege.'" *

In 1858, Mr. Lincoln was nominated by the Republicans as candidate for the United-States Senate. Mr. Douglas was his rival on the Democratic ticket. Both stumped the State, and finally held personal debates with each other without personal animosity on the different political views they held. Judge Douglas had the grace, at Springfield, to say, "I take great pleasure in bearing testimony to the fact that Mr. Lincoln is a kind-hearted, amiable, good-natured gentleman, with whom no man has a right to pick a quarrel, even if he wanted one. He is a worthy gentleman. I have known him for twenty-five years; and there is no better citizen, and no kinder-hearted man. He is a fine lawyer, possesses high ability; and there is no objection to him, except the monstrous revolutionary doctrines with which he is identified."

In July, 1858, Lincoln threw down the gauntlet, which Douglas lifted, and seven debates followed, at Ottawa, Freeport, Jonesborough, Charleston, Galesburg, Quincy, and Alton. They are said to be unsurpassed in campaign

* Raymond's "Life of Lincoln."

annals for eloquence, ability, adroitness, or comprehensiveness. Often these rival candidates travelled in the same car or carriage, manifesting personal good feeling, yet each contending fearlessly for the mastery when they entered the gladiatorial area for debate.

During this campaign, Mr. Lincoln paid a tribute to the Declaration of Independence, which should be read by all who revere his memory: "These communities, (the thirteen colonies) by their representatives in old Indendence Hall, said to the world of men, 'We hold these truths to be self-evident, that all men are born equal; that they are endowed by their Creator with inalienable rights; that among these are life, liberty, and the pursuit of happiness.' This was their majestic interpretation of the economy of the universe. This was their lofty and wise and noble understanding of the justice of the Creator to his creatures. Yes, gentlemen, to all his creatures, to the whole great family of man. In their enlightened belief, nothing stamped with the divine image and likeness was sent into the world to be trodden on and degraded and imbruted by its fellows. They grasped not only the race of men then living, but they reached forward and seized upon the farthest posterity. They created a beacon to guide their children and their children's children, and the countless myriads who should inhabit the earth in other ages. Wise statesmen as they were, they knew the tendency of prosperity to breed tyrants; and so they established these self-evident truths, that when, in the distant future, some man, some faction, some interest, should set up the doctrine, that none but rich men, or none but white men, or none but Anglo-Saxon white men, were entitled to life, liberty, and the pursuit of happiness, their posterity might look up again to the Declaration of Independence, and take courage to renew the battle which their fathers began; so that truth and justice and mercy, and all the humane and Christian virtues, might not be extinguished from the land; so that no man would hereafter dare to limit and circumscribe the great principles on which the temple of Liberty was being built.

"Now, my countrymen, if you have been taught doctrines conflicting with the great land-marks of the Declaration of Independence; if you have listened to suggestions which would take away from its grandeur and mutilate the fair symmetry of its proportions; if you have been inclined to believe that all men are not created equal in those inalienable rights enumerated by our charter of liberty, — let me entreat you to come back; return to the fountain whose waters spring close by the blood of the Revolution. Think nothing of me, take no thought for the political fate of any man whomsoever, but come back to the truths that are in the Declaration of Independence.

"You may do any thing with me that you choose, if you will but heed these sacred principles; you may not only defeat me for the Senate, but you may take me and put me to death. While pretending no indifference to earthly honors, I *do claim* to be actuated in this contest by something higher than an anxiety for office. I charge you to drop every paltry and insignificant thought for any man's success. It is nothing; I am nothing; Judge Douglas is nothing. *But do not destroy that immortal emblem of humanity, — the Declaration of American Independence.*"

Though it is not designed to enlarge this volume by the publication of many of our late President's speeches or letters, the following eloquent outburst of patriotism and devotion to principle must not be omitted. It is the closing part of a speech made in December, 1839.

"Many free countries have lost their liberties, and ours may lose hers; but if she shall, may it be my proudest plume, not that I was the last to desert her, but that I never deserted her! I know that the great volcano at Washington, aroused and directed by the evil spirit that reigns there, is belching forth the lava of political corruption in a current broad and deep, which is sweeping with frightful velocity over the whole length and breadth of the land, bidding fair to leave unscathed no green spot or living thing; while on its bosom are riding, like demons on the waves of hell, the imps of the evil spirit, and fiendishly torturing and taunting all those who dare resist its destroying course with the hopelessness of their efforts; and knowing this, I cannot deny that all may be swept away. Broken by it I too may be; bow to it I never will. The probability that we may fall in the struggle ought not to deter us from the support of a cause which we deem to be just. It shall not deter me. If ever I feel the soul within me elevate and expand to those dimensions not wholly unworthy the Almighty Architect, it is when I contemplate the cause of my country deserted by all the world besides, and I, standing alone, hurling defiance at her victorious oppressors. And here, without contemplating consequences, before high heaven, and in the face of the whole world, I swear eternal fidelity to the just cause, as I deem it, of the land of my life, my liberty, and my love. And who that thinks with me will not adopt the oath that I take? Let none falter who thinks he is right, and we may succeed. But if, after all, we shall fall, be it so. We shall have the proud consolation of saying to our conscience, and to the departed shade of our country's freedom, that the course approved by our judgments and adored by our hearts, in disaster, in chains, in torture, and in death, we never faltered in defending."

One of the greatest speeches of his life was made by Mr. Lincoln in New York, at the Cooper Institute, on the 27th of February, 1860, before a crowded house; the venerable poet, William Cullen Bryant, presiding, and introducing the speaker in highly complimentary terms. It is too long for place on these pages, and its unity so perfect, that it is not easy to quote from it. It was eminently patriotic, and did much toward securing for him the favor of the New-York Republicans in the hour of nomination for the Presidency.

Some writer has given the following pen-portrait of President Lincoln, which is believed to be correct: —

"Mr. Lincoln stands six feet and four inches high in his stockings. His frame is not muscular, but gaunt and wiry; his arms are long, but not unreasonably so for a person of his height; his lower limbs are not disproportioned to his body. In walking, his gait, though firm, is never brisk. He steps slowly and deliberately, almost always with his head inclined forward, and his hands clasped behind his back. In matters of dress he is by no means precise. Always clean, he is never fashionable; he is careless, but not slovenly. In manner he is remarkably cordial, and, at the same time, simple. His politeness is always sincere, but never elaborate and oppressive. A warm shake of the hand, and a warmer smile of recognition, are his methods of greeting his friends. At rest, his features, though those of a man of mark, are not such as belong to a handsome man; but when his fine dark gray eyes are lighted up by any emotion, and his features begin their play, he would be chosen from among a crowd as one who had in him not only the kindly sentiments which women love, but the heavier

5*

metal of which full-grown men and presidents are made. His hair is black, and, though thin, is wiry. His head sits well on his shoulders, but beyond that it defies description. It nearer resembles that of Clay than that of Webster; but it is unlike either. It is very large, and, phrenologically, well-proportioned, betokening power in all its developments. A slightly Roman nose, a wide-cut mouth, and a dark complexion, with the appearance of having been weather-beaten, complete the description.

"In his personal habits, Mr. Lincoln is simple as a child. He loves a good dinner, and eats with the appetite which goes with a great brain; but his food is plain and nutritious. He never drinks intoxicating liquors of any sort, not even a glass of wine. He is not addicted to the use of tobacco in any shape. He never was accused of a licentious act in all his life. He never uses profane language."

How would the heart of Lincoln's pious mother have rejoiced, could she have foreseen such a record of her son's spotless character and blameless life!

Still another writer pictures his manner in speaking: "As a speaker, he is ready, precise, and fluent. His manner before a popular assembly is as he pleases to make it, being either superlatively ludicrous or very impressive. He employs but little gesticulation, but, when he desires to make a point, produces a shrug of his shoulders, an elevation of his eyebrows, a depression of his mouth, and a general malformation of countenance so comically awkward, that it never fails to bring down the house. His enunciation is slow and emphatic; and his voice, though sharp and powerful, at times has a frequent tendency to dwindle into a shrill and unpleasant sound. But, as before stated, the peculiar characteristic of his delivery is the remarkable mobility of his features, the frequent contortions of which excite a merriment his words could not produce."

A distinguished scholar, who heard him debate with Mr. Douglas, says, "He then proceeded to defend the Republican party. Here he charged Mr. Douglas with doing nothing for freedom; with disregarding the rights and interests of the colored man; and for about forty minutes he spoke with a power that we have seldom heard equalled. There was a grandeur in his thoughts, a comprehensiveness in his arguments, and a binding force in his conclusions, which were perfectly irresistible. The vast throng were silent as death: every eye was fixed upon the speaker, and all gave him serious attention. He was the tall man eloquent: his countenance glowed with animation, and his eye glistened with an intelligence that made it lustrous. He was no longer awkward and ungainly, but graceful, bold, commanding."

Here the chapter narrating the struggles and successes of his manhood, previous to his entering on his great work, may fittingly close. It has been conclusively shown that the growing man was preparing for the advancing era. Bishop Simpson stated in his funeral address, that, "as early as 1839, Mr. Lincoln presented resolutions in the Legislature asking for emancipation in the District of Columbia, when, with but rare exceptions, the whole popular mind of his State was opposed to the measure. From that hour he was a steady and uniform friend of humanity, and was preparing for the conflict of later years."

Who cannot see God's hand in all these events, though rapidly traced, as the hour and the man approached each other? The scroll of Time is fast unrolling; and as every day prophecy becomes history, we should learn lessons of patient hope, and humble, earnest, rejoicing faith; for —

> "Blind unbelief is sure to err,
> And scan His work in vain:
> God is his own interpreter,
> And he will make it plain."

CHAPTER IV.

CALLED TO THE PRESIDENTIAL CHAIR.

"The man whom Heaven appoints
To govern others should himself first learn
To bend his passions to the sway of reason."
THOMSON'S TANCRED AND SIGISMUNDA.

"Then Samuel took the horn of oil, and anointed him in the midst of his brethren; and the Spirit of the Lord came upon David from that day forward."
1 SAM. xvi. 13.

THE prepared man now moved toward the appointed place of labor. The hour of destiny struck in Chicago on the 18th of May, 1860, when the Republican National Convention met "in an immense building, which the people of Chicago had put up for the purpose, called the Wigwam. There were four hundred and sixty-five delegates. The city was filled with earnest men who had gathered to press the claims of their favorite candidates, and the halls and corridors of all the hotels swarmed and buzzed with an eager crowd, in and out of which darted or pushed or wormed their way the various leaders of party politics." *

Mr. Lincoln was then at his home in Springfield. With a not improper anxiety to hear the result of the Convention, he called at the telegraph-office, and there learned how the first and second ballots resulted. He then left, and, going to the office of the "State Journal," sat there quietly conversing with some friends, when a boy placed a note in his hand. It was the announcement of his

* Raymond's "Life of Lincoln."

nomination on the third ballot. He looked at it silently, while the friends around him shouted in triumph; and then, putting it into his pocket, with characteristic calmness he said, in his own peculiar way, "There is a little woman down at our house would like to hear this; I'll go down and tell her;" and immediately returned to his home.

The next day brought to Springfield the Committee appointed by the Convention to inform Mr. Lincoln officially of his nomination. They were escorted to his house by a large concourse of citizens. One * who was present on that occasion, and will never forget that memorable visit to the plain, white, two-story wooden

LINCOLN'S HOME IN SPRINGFIELD.

house, on the corner of two streets, where the unpretending nominee received his official visitors, stated to the writer of these pages that no refreshments were provided save iced-water; and that when citizens of

* C. C. Coffin, Esq.,—"Carleton" of the "Boston Journal."

Springfield, apprising Mr. Lincoln of the coming Committee, asked him to furnish them with wine, &c., as was customary, he refused, saying he never used liquors himself, and could not give them to others: they insisted on furnishing some themselves; but the noble man answered characteristically, "I will not permit my friends to do in my house what I will not do myself." So temperance principles triumphed, and those citizens could only "put the cup to their neighbors' lip" by taking them afterward to a hotel, where all who wished strong drink could be gratified.

The President of the Convention was spokesman for the Committee, and in a brief speech informed the host of his nomination. With an expression half sad, half dignified, Mr. Lincoln heard the words; and, after a short pause of reflection, he answered: —

"Mr. Chairman and Gentlemen of the Committee, —

"I tender to you, and through you to the Republican National Convention, and all the people represented in it, my profoundest thanks for the high honor done me, which you now formally announce. Deeply and even painfully sensible of the great responsibility which is inseparable from this high honor, — a responsibility which I could almost wish had fallen upon some one of the far more eminent men and experienced statesmen whose distinguished names were before the Convention, — I shall, by your leave, consider more fully the resolutions of the Convention denominated the platform, and without any unnecessary or unreasonable delay respond to you, Mr. Chairman, in writing, not doubting that the platform will be found satisfactory, and the nomination gratefully accepted. And now I will not longer defer the pleasure of taking you and each of you by the hand."

As one incident of this interesting occasion, it is said that "tall Judge Kelly of Pennsylvania, who was one of the Committee, and who is himself a great many feet high, had meanwhile been eying Mr. Lincoln's lofty form with a mixture of admiration, and very likely jealousy: this had not escaped Mr. Lincoln, and, as he shook hands with the judge, he inquired, 'What is your height?'—'Six feet three: what is yours, Mr. Lincoln?' 'Six feet four.'

"'Then,' said the judge, 'Pennsylvania bows to Illinois. My dear man, for years my heart has been aching for a President that I could *look up to*, and I've found him at last in a land where we thought there were none but *little* giants.'" *

On the 23d of the month, Mr. Lincoln replied formally, by letter, to the official announcement of his nomination, in these words:—

"Hon. GEORGE ASHMUN.

"Sir,—I accept the nomination tendered me by the Convention over which you presided, of which I am formally apprised in a letter of yourself and others acting as a Committee of the Convention for that purpose. The declaration of principles and sentiments which accompanies your letter meets my approval, and it shall be my care not to violate it or disregard it in any part. Imploring the assistance of Divine Providence, and with due regard to the views and feelings of all who were represented in the Convention, to the rights of all the States and Territories and people of the nation, to the inviolability of the Constitution, and the perpetual union, harmony, and prosperity of all, I am most happy to co-

* Raymond's "Life of Lincoln."

operate for the practical success of the principles declared by the Convention.

"Your obliged friend and fellow-citizen,

"ABRAHAM LINCOLN."

The enthusiasm of the Republicans during the ensuing presidential campaign was very great, scarcely equalled even in the log-cabin days of "Tippecanoe and Tyler too;" and, as one after another of the Northern and Western States declared the Chicago nominee to be their choice, the wildest demonstrations of joy were exhibited in torch-light processions, illuminations, &c., all over the loyal portion of the country. The Quakers of Pennsylvania were moved from their position of "eminent gravity" on this occasion, and polled an overwhelming vote for the champion of liberty; and the Quaker poet — who stands second to none in America — told the triumph in tuneful numbers.*

The solid phalanx of earnest men who had resolved that freedom should reign in America formed a body of

* It was the privilege of the writer to prepare, as a portion of the street decorations on the premises of Mr. S. D. Herrick, on the occasion of a jubilee illumination in Beverly, Mass., one line of Whittier's poem, in gigantic lettering; viz., "For Lincoln goes in when the Quakers come out." The whole poem was read at a Republican meeting in Georgetown, Mass., and was as follows: —

"Not vainly we waited, and counted the hours;
The buds of our hope have burst out into flowers.
No room for misgiving; no loop-hole of doubt:
We've heard from the Keystone! The Quakers are out!

The plot has exploded; we've found out the trick;
The bribe goes a-begging; the fusion won't stick:
When the Wide-Awake lanterns are shining about,
The rogues stay at home, and the true men come out!

The good State has broken the córds for her spun;
Her oil-springs and water won't fuse into one;

nearly two millions of voters, who carried for Mr. Lincoln the electoral votes of the States of Maine, New Hampshire, Vermont, Massachusetts, Rhode Island, Connecticut, New York, Pennsylvania, Ohio, Indiana, Illinois, Michigan, Iowa, Wisconsin, Minnesota, and California.

Already the mutterings of the coming storm were to be heard along the horizon. A pusillanimous President sat helpless in the White House, while seceding States unrighteously possessed themselves of forts and other Government property, and began to prepare for civil war. Never nation needed a leader more. God saw our necessity. It was his glorious opportunity. He saw our need of a pillar of fire in the night of war fast settling down upon us; and, lo! Abraham Lincoln "stood before us, a man of the people. He was thoroughly American; had never crossed the sea, had never been spoiled by English insularity or French dissipation; a quiet native, aboriginal man, as an acorn from the oak; no aping of foreigners, no frivolous accomplishments; Kentuckian-born, working on a farm; a flatboat-man, a captain in the Black-Hawk War, a country lawyer, a representative in the rural Legislature of Illinois, — on such modest foundations the broad structure of his fame was laid. How slowly, and yet by happily prepared steps, he came to his place!" *

One eloquent eulogist † thus pictured the people's choice: "In person he was tall and rugged, with little

The Dutchman has seasoned with freedom his krout;
And slow, late, but certain, the Quakers are out!

Give the flag to the winds! set the hills all aflame!
Make way for the man with the patriarch's name!
Away with misgiving, away with all doubt!
For LINCOLN goes in when the Quakers come out!"

* R. W. Emerson. † Hon. Charles Sumner.

resemblance to any historic portrait, unless he might seem in one respect to justify the epithet which was given to an early English monarch. His countenance had even more of rugged strength than his person. Perhaps the quality which struck the most at first sight was his simplicity of manners and conversation, without form or ceremony of any kind, beyond that among neighbors. His hand-writing had the same simplicity. It was as clear as that of Washington, but less florid. Each had been a surveyor, and was perhaps indebted to this experience. But the son of the Western pioneer was more simple in nature, and the man appeared in the autograph. That integrity which has become a proverb belonged to the same quality. The most perfect honesty must be the most perfect simplicity. The words by which an ancient Roman was described belong to him: *Vitâ innocentissimus, proposito sanctissimus.* He was naturally humane, inclined to pardon, and never remembering the hard things said against him. He was always good to the poor, and in his dealings with them was full of those 'kind little words which are of the same blood as great and holy deeds.' Such a character awakened instinctively the sympathy of the people. They saw his fellow-feeling with them, and felt the kinship. With him as President, the idea of republican institutions, where no place is too high for the humblest, was perpetually manifest, so that his simple presence was like a proclamation of the equality of all men."

Such pen-pictures of this great and good man are often to be met, and will continually be drawn by poets, eulogists, and historians. One of those invaluable newspaper correspondents, who like his co-laborers aided to give the waiting North a true panorama of events from time to time, thus speaks of President Lincoln: "Our interview left no grotesque recollections of the President lounging, his huge hands and feet, great mouth, or angular features. We remembered rather the ineffable tenderness which shone through his gentle eyes, his childlike ingenuousness, his utter integrity, and his love of country. Ignorant of etiquette and conventionalities, without the graces of form or manner, his great reluctance to give pain, his beautiful regard for the feelings of others, made him —

> 'Worthy to bear without reproach
> The grand old name of gentleman.'

Strong without symmetry, humorous without levity, religious without cant; tender, merciful, forgiving; a profound believer in divine love, an earnest worker for human brotherhood, — Abe Lincoln was perhaps the best contribution which America has made to history."*

As another most eloquent eulogist † said before the General Assembly of Connecticut, " His greatness is the most original and *bizarre* in the world's history, shaped after no model, suggesting as a compact whole no pattern, no parallel, . . . and can only be loosely described as composed of great simplicity, great naturalness, great *bonhomie*, great shrewdness, great strength, great devotion, great equanimity, and great success, on the greatest theatre ever offered to such qualities for exhibition. . . . Ennobled by no patent but that of nature, with no diploma but his record, crowned as it were with the wild flowers of the forest, and with all its flavor and freshness upon him, he walks into the surprised Pantheon of the world's great men, a large grotesque backwoodsman, but with credentials to admission which

* A. D. Richardson's "The Secret Service, — the Field, Dungeon, and Escape."

† Hon. H. C. Deming.

cannot be challenged or disallowed; like the hirsute and half-naked Brennus striding into the grave and reverend decorum of a Roman senate; like Hans Luther's plebeian and beetle-browed son confronting the stoled, mitred, and ermined Diet of Charles the Fifth; like a red-nosed, cropped, and mail-clad Cromwell, shuffling through the silken splendors, the Vandyke dresses, the perfumed love-locks, and the fastidious etiquette, of outraged Whitehall; like St. Artegans' iron soldier, marching with his invincible flail into the startled and shrinking ranks of vulnerable and pain-suffering warriors."

One aim of this volume is to give a true picture of Abraham Lincoln as a man, and the concurrent testimony of various contemporaries is exceedingly valuable. The "New-York World," which, while he lived, was ever opposed to his cause and policy, thus spoke of the people's choice when death had set its seal upon his virtues:—

"If we look for the elements of character which have contributed to the extraordinary and constantly growing popularity of Mr. Lincoln, we have not far to seek. The kindly, companionable, jovial turn of his disposition, free from every taint of affectation, puerile vanity, or *parvenu* insolence, conveyed a strong impression of worth, sense, and solidity, as well as goodness of heart. He never disclosed the slightest symptom that he was dazzled or elated by his great position, or that it was incumbent upon him to be anybody but plain Abraham Lincoln. This was in infinitely better taste than would have been any attempt to put on manners that did not sit easily upon his training and habits, under the false notion that he would be supporting the dignity of his office. No offence in manners is so intolerable as affectation, nor any thing so vulgar as a soul haunted by an uneasy consciousness of vulgarity. Mr. Lincoln's freedom from any such upstart affectations was one of the good points of his character: it betokened his genuineness and sincerity."

On the 11th of February, 1861, the President elect left his home in Springfield for Washington. A vast crowd attended him at the depot; and before the cars started he thus addressed a few farewell words to his neighbors and friends: —

"MY FRIENDS, — No one not in my position can appreciate the sadness I feel at this parting. To this people I owe all that I am. Here I have lived more than a quarter of a century. Here my children were born, and here one of them lies buried. I know not how soon I shall see you again. A duty devolves upon me which is perhaps greater than that which has devolved upon any other man since the days of Washington. He never would have succeeded except for the aid of Divine Providence, upon which he at all times relied. I feel that I cannot succeed without the same divine aid which sustained him, and in the same Almighty Being I place my reliance for support; and I hope you, my friends, will all pray that I may receive that divine assistance, without which I cannot succeed, but with which success is certain. Again I bid you all an affectionate farewell."

All along the route to the Capitol, multitudes assembled at the railway stations to greet him, and on several occasions he addressed them in few but happily chosen words.

At Toledo, in response to continual calls, he appeared on the platform, and said, "I am leaving you on an errand of national importance, attended, as you are aware, with considerable difficulties. Let us believe, as some poet has expressed it, —

'Behind the cloud the sun is shining still.'

I bid you an affectionate farewell."

At Indianapolis, Mr. Lincoln was welcomed by the Governor of the State, and escorted by a procession composed of the Legislature, municipal authorities, military, and firemen. On reaching the hotel, he addressed the people in his own homely and humorous but sensible manner, giving some intimation of the policy he would pursue: —

"Fellow-Citizens of the State of Indiana, — I am here to thank you for this magnificent welcome, and still more for the very generous support given by your State to that political cause, which, I think, is the true and just cause of the whole country and the whole world. Solomon says, 'There is a time to keep silence;' and when men wrangle by the mouth, with no certainty that they mean the same thing while using the same words, it perhaps were as well if they would keep silence.

"The words 'coercion' and 'invasion' are much used in these days, and often with some temper and hot blood. Let us make sure, if we can, that we do not misunderstand the meaning of those who use them. Let us get the exact definition of these words, not from dictionaries, but from the men themselves, who certainly deprecate the things they would represent by the use of the words. What, then, is 'coercion'? what is 'invasion'? Would the marching of an army into South Carolina, without the consent of her people, and with hostile intent toward them, be invasion? I certainly think it would, and it would be coercion also if the South Carolinians were forced to submit. But if the United States should merely hold and retake its own forts and other property, and collect the duties on foreign importations, or even withhold the mails from places where they were habitually violated, would any or all of these things be invasion or coercion? Do our professed lovers of the Union, who spitefully resolve that they will resist coercion and invasion, understand that such things as these, on the part of the United States, would be coercion or invasion of a State? If so, their idea of means to preserve the object of their great affection would seem to be exceedingly thin and airy. If sick, the little pills of the homœopathist would be much too large for it to swallow. In their view, the Union, as a family relation, would seem to be no regular marriage, but rather a sort of free-love arrangement, to be maintained on passional attraction.

"By the way, in what consists the special sacredness of a State? I speak not of the position assigned to a State in the Union by the Constitution, for that is a bond we all recognize. That position, however, a State cannot carry out of the Union with it. I speak of that assumed primary right of a State to rule all which is less than itself, and to ruin all which is larger than itself. If a State and a county, in a given case, should be equal in number of inhabitants, in what, as a matter of principle, is the State better than the county? Would an exchange of name be an exchange of rights? Upon what principle, upon what rightful principle, may a State, being no more than one-fiftieth part of the nation in soil and population, break up the nation, and then coerce a proportionably large sub-division of itself in the most arbitrary way? What mysterious right to play tyrant is conferred on a district or county, with its people, by simply calling it a State? Fellow-citizens, I am not asserting any thing: I am merely asking questions for you to consider. And now allow me to bid you farewell."

At Cincinnati, the President elect received a most enthusiastic welcome. He was escorted to the Burnet House by the Mayor of the city, who addressed him in words of welcome, to which he made a fitting response.

At Columbus also he received a cordial welcome, and spoke briefly. At Steubenville he also made a brief address. He spoke also at Pittsburg and Cleveland; but the limits of this volume forbid the insertion of all these speeches. Ex-President Fillmore headed the citizen-host who greeted him at Buffalo, and the Mayor welcomed him in words. At Albany he was conducted to the Capitol, and welcomed by Gov. Morgan. At Poughkeepsie he was welcomed by the Mayor, and also in New York. It is said that the reception in that commercial metropolis was "a most imposing demonstration: places of business were generally closed, and hundreds of thousands were in the streets." At Trenton he tarried a few hours, and visited both houses of the Legislature. He addressed the Senate as follows:—

"Mr. President, and Gentlemen of the
Senate of the State of New Jersey,—

"I am very grateful to you for the honorable reception of which I have been the object. I cannot but remember the place that New Jersey holds in our early history. In the early Revolutionary struggle, few of the States among the old Thirteen had more of the battle-fields of the country within its limits than old New Jersey. May I be pardoned, if, upon this occasion, I mention that away back in my childhood, the earliest days of my being able to read, I got hold of a small book,—such a one as few of the younger members have ever seen,—Weems's 'Life of Washington'? I remember all the accounts there given of the battle-fields and struggles for the liberty of the country; and none fixed themselves upon my imagination so deeply as the struggle here at Trenton, New Jersey. The crossing of the river, the contest with the Hessians, the great hardships endured at that time, all fixed themselves on my memory more than any single Revolutionary event; and you all know, for you have all been boys, how these early impressions last longer than any others. I recollect thinking then, boy even though I was, that there must have been something more than common that those men struggled for. I am exceedingly anxious that that thing which they struggled for; that something, even more than national independence; that something, that held out a great promise to all the people of the world in all time to come, — I am exceedingly anxious that this Union, the Constitution, and the liberties of the people, shall be perpetuated in accordance with the original idea for which that struggle was made; and I shall be happy indeed if I shall be a humble instrument, in the hands of the Almighty and of this his almost chosen people, for perpetuating the object of that great struggle. You give me this reception, as I understand, without distinction of party. I learn that this body is composed of a majority of gentlemen, who, in the exercise of their best judgment in the choice of a chief magistrate, did not think I was the man. I understand, nevertheless, that they came forward here to greet me as the constitutional President of the United States; as citizens of the United States, to meet the man, who, for the time being, is the representative man of the nation, united by a purpose to perpetuate the Union and liberties of the people. As such, I accept this reception more gratefully than I could do did I believe it was tendered to me as an individual."

Mr. Lincoln then addressed the Assembly; and after repeating, in substance, some things in his previous speech, continued: "You, Mr. Speaker, have well said that this is the time when the bravest and wisest look with doubt and awe upon the aspect presented by our national affairs. Under these circumstances, you will readily see why I should not speak in detail of the course I shall deem it best to pursue. It is proper that I should avail myself of all the information and all the time at my command, in order that, when the time arrives in which I must speak officially, I shall be able to take the ground which I deem the best and safest, and from which I may have no occasion to swerve. I shall endeavor to take the ground I deem most just to the North, the East, the West, the South, and the whole country. I take it, I hope, in good temper, — certainly with no malice towards any section. I shall do all that may be in my power to promote a peaceful settlement of all our difficulties. The man does not live who is more devoted to peace than I am; none who would do more to preserve it. But it may be necessary to put the foot firmly down; and if I do my duty, and do it right, you will sustain me, will you not? Received as I am by the members of a Legislature, the majority of whom do not agree with me in political sentiment, I trust that I may have their assistance in piloting the Ship of State through this voyage, surrounded by perils as it is; for, if it should suffer shipwreck now, there will be no pilot needed for another voyage."

On arriving at Philadelphia, the words of welcome and response were again uttered; and the next morning Mr. Lincoln visited the old "Independence Hall" for the purpose of raising the national flag over it. Here he was warmly welcomed, and spoke as follows: —

"I am filled with deep emotion at finding myself standing here in this place, where were collected the wisdom, the patriotism, the devotion to principle, from which sprang the institutions under which we live. You have kindly suggested to me that in my hands is the task of restoring peace to the present distracted condition of the country. I can say in return, sir, that all the political sentiments I entertain have been drawn, so far as I have been able to draw them, from the sentiments which originated, and were given to the world, from this hall. I have never had a feeling politically that did not spring from the sentiments embodied in the Declaration of Independence. I have often pondered over the dangers which were incurred by the men who assembled here, and framed and adopted that Declaration of Independence. I have pondered over the toils that were endured by the officers and soldiers of the army who achieved that independence. I have often inquired of myself what great principle or idea it was that kept this confederacy so long together. It was not the mere matter of the separation of the colonies from the motherland, but that sentiment in the Declaration of Independence which gave liberty, not alone to the people of this country, but, I hope, to the world for all future time. It was that which gave promise, that, in due time, the weight would be lifted from the shoulders of all men. This is a sentiment embodied in the Declaration of Independence. Now, my friends, can this country be saved upon this basis? If it can, I will consider myself one of the happiest men in the world if I can help to save it. If it cannot be saved upon that principle, it will be truly awful. But if this country cannot be saved without giving up that principle, I was about to say I would rather be assassinated on this spot than surrender it. Now, in my view of the present aspect of affairs, there need be no bloodshed or war. There is no necessity for it. I am not in favor of such a course; and I may say, in advance, that there will be no blood shed unless it be forced upon the Government, and then it will be forced to act in self-defence.

"My friends, this is wholly an unexpected speech, and I did not expect to be called upon to say a word when I came here. I supposed it was merely to do something towards raising the flag. I may, therefore, have said something indiscreet. I have said nothing but what I am willing to live by, and, if it be the pleasure of Almighty God, to die by."

The party then proceeded to a platform in front of the State House; and there Mr. Lincoln made a brief speech, stating his willingness to comply with the request to raise the flag, and alluded to the original flag of thirteen stars, saying that "the number had increased as time rolled on, and each star added to the prosperity of the nation.

"The future," he added, "is in the hands of the people. It is on such an occasion as this that we can reason together, and re-affirm our devotion to the country and the principles of the Declaration of Independence. Let us make up our minds, that, when we do put a new star upon our banner, it shall be a fixed one, never to be dimmed by the horrors of war, but brightened by the contentment and prosperity of peace. Let us go on to extend the area of our usefulness, add star upon star, until their light shall shine upon five hundred millions of a free and happy people." Mr. Lincoln then raised the flag to the top of the staff.

Shortly after, he and his party left for Harrisburg. Here he addressed the Legislature; and, referring to the morning's experience, said, "Our friends there had provided a magnificent flag of the country. They had arranged it so that I was given the honor of raising it to the head of its staff; and, when it went up, I was pleased that it went to its place by the strength of my own feeble arm. When, according to the arrangement, the cord was pulled, and it flaunted gloriously to the wind without an accident in the bright glowing sunshine of the morning, I could not help hoping that there was, in the entire success of that beautiful ceremony, at least something of an omen of what is to come; nor could I help feeling then, as I often have felt, in the whole of that proceeding, I was a very humble instrument. I had not provided the flag; I had not made arrangements for elevating it to its place; I had applied but a very small portion of my feeble strength in raising it. In the whole transaction, I was in the hands of the people who had arranged it; and, if I can have the same generous co-operation of the people of the nation, I think the flag of our country may be kept flaunting gloriously!"

Those who lived to see the events of the four years in which President Lincoln guided the nation to victory and freedom can recognize the omen of which he spoke, as gloriously fulfilled.

He did not speak again in public till he reached Washington. At Philadelphia, information was communicated to him of a plot which was on foot to assassinate him in Baltimore. The existence of such a plot had been suspected before. Threats had been freely made by the more fanatical Southern men that he would never reach Washington alive. An attempt was made to throw from the track the car in which he was riding on his journey through Ohio; and, just as he was leaving Cincinnati, a hand-grenade was found to have been secreted on board the cars. Investigations were set on foot which revealed the fact that a small gang of assassins, under the leadership of an Italian, who assumed the name of Orsini, had undertaken to do the work of the slaveholders by murdering Mr. Lincoln as he passed through Baltimore.

"The only precaution which he took against this attack was to leave Harrisburg one train earlier than had been expected. He thus passed through Baltimore in the night, and arrived in Washington on the morning of Saturday, the 23d of February, where his safe arrival was greeted with joy by his friends, and ill-concealed disappointment by his enemies. The threats against his life were continued; and but for the watchfulness and determination of his friends, and the care and military preparations of Gen. Scott, it is quite probable that his inauguration would never have taken place." *

A correspondent of the "New-York Herald" thus narrates the occurrences of the memorable day:—

"On the day of his arrival in Washington he dined with Mr. Seward, called on the President; and at ten minutes before nine, P.M., he returned to his hotel, and was received by an enthusiastic crowd, who greeted him as though he was their father and their life. Some were old men, and some were old and young ladies. They reflected the general feeling, that in Mr. Lincoln rests the future hope of the Government and the Union.

"Mr. Lincoln passed through the long parlor-hall, thronged with the *élite* and fashion of the national metropolis, shaking hands as fast as he could on his right and left with the ladies and gentlemen, so intensely interested, that he forgot even to take his hat off, which was excused by a looker-on, who remarked that it was new, and outshined the crowd.

"At nine o'clock, according to previous arrangement, Mr. Lincoln received the Peace Congress. The members

* Henry J. Raymond's "Life of Lincoln."

formed in procession in the hall where they met, and proceeded to the reception parlor. Ex-President Tyler, and Governor Chase of Ohio, led the van. The latter introduced Mr. Tyler: Mr. Lincoln received him with all the respect due to his position. The several delegates were then presented to Mr. Lincoln by Gov. Chase in the usual manner.

"The greatest curiosity was manifested to witness Mr. Lincoln's first reception in Washington. The most marvellous thing that occurred was the manifestation by Mr. Lincoln of a most wonderful memory. It will be remembered that the convention is composed of many men, who, although distinguished in their time, have until very lately not been very much known. Each member was introduced by his last name; but, in nine cases out of ten, Mr. Lincoln would promptly recall their entire name, no matter how many initials it contained. In several instances he recited the historical reminiscences of families. In short, he understands the material of the Peace Congress.

"When the tall Gen. Doniphan of Missouri was introduced, Mr. Lincoln had to look up to catch Doniphan's eye. He immediately inquired, 'Is this Doniphan, who made that splendid march across the plains, and swept the swift Camanches before him?'—'I commanded the expedition across the plains,' modestly responded the general.

'"Then you have come up to the standard of my expectations,' rejoined Mr. Lincoln.

"After the reception of the Peace Congress was concluded, a large number of citizens were presented. Mr. Lincoln was then notified that the ante-rooms and main parlors of the hotel were filled with ladies who desired to pay their respects; to which the President-elect very promptly consented. The ladies then passed in review, each being introduced by the gentleman who accompanied her. Mr. Lincoln underwent the new ordeal with much good humor.

"At ten o'clock, Mr. Buchanan's Cabinet called, and paid their respects, in response to Mr. Lincoln's *coup d'état* at the White House in the morning. Their reception was very pleasant.

"It may be truly said that Mr. Lincoln's first day in Washington as President-elect has been a decided success. Democrats as well as Republicans are pleased with him; and the ladies, who thought he was awkward at first sight, changed their opinion, and now declare him 'a very pleasant, sociable gentleman, and not bad-looking by any means.'"

The 4th of March, 1861, arrived, Inauguration Day. It was somewhat cloudy and cool in the morning, but afterwards seemed like May, bright and genial.

"The ceremonies at the inauguration of Mr. Lincoln were in some respects the most brilliant and imposing ever witnessed at Washington. Nearly twenty well-drilled military companies of the District, comprising a force of more than two thousand men, were on parade. Georgetown sent companies of cavalry, infantry, and artillery, of fine appearance. The troops stationed at the City Hall and Willard's Hotel became objects of attraction to vast numbers of both sexes. At noon the Senate Committee called upon President Buchanan, who proceeded with them to Willard's Hotel to receive the President-elect. The party thus composed, joined by other distinguished citizens, then proceeded in open carriages along the avenue at a moderate pace, with military in front and rear, and thousands of private citizens in carriages, on horseback and on foot, crowding the broad street. The Capitol was reached by passing up on the north side of the grounds, and the party entered the building by the northern door over a temporary planked walk. During the hour and a half previous to the arrival of President Buchanan and the President-elect in the Senate Chamber, that hall presented a gayer spectacle than ever before. The usual desks of the senators had been removed, and concentric lines of ornamented chairs set for the dignitaries of this and other lands with which this country was in bonds of amity and friendship. The inner half-circle on the extreme left was occupied by the members of the cabinets of Mr. Buchanan and Mr. Lincoln, mingled together, and farther on by senators. The concentric circle farther back was filled with senators. The next half-circle immediately in the rear of that occupied by the ministers were the secretaries and attachés. The half-circles on the left, corresponding to those occupied by the corps diplomatique, furnished places for senators and governors of States and Territories. Outside of all, on both sides, stood—for there was no further room for seats—the members of the House of Representatives and chief officers of the executive bureaus. The galleries all round the Senate were occupied by ladies.

"At a quarter-past one o'clock, the President of the United States and the President-elect entered the Senate Chamber, preceded by Senator Foote and the marshal of the District of Columbia, and followed by Senators Baker and Pearce. They took seats immediately in front of the clerk's desk, facing outward; President Buchanan having the President-elect on his right, and the senators equally distributed right and left.

"In a few minutes, Vice-President Hamlin, who had been previously installed, ordered the reading of the order of procession to the platform on the east of the Capitol; and the line was formed, the Marshal of the District of Columbia leading. Then followed Chief Justice Taney and the Judges of the Supreme Court, the Sergeant-at-arms of the Senate, the Committee of Arrangements of the Senate, the President of the United States and the President-elect, Vice-President of the United States, and Senate, the members of the diplomatic corps, governors of State and Territories, and members of the House of Representatives. In this order the procession marched to the platform erected in the usual position over the main steps on the east front of the Capitol, where a temporary covering had been placed to protect the President-elect from possible rain during the reading of his inaugural address. The greater part of an hour was occupied in seating the procession on the platform, and in the delivery of the address of Mr. Lincoln, which he read with a clear, loud, and distinct voice, quite intelligible to at least ten thousand persons below him. At the close of the address, Mr. Lincoln took the oath of office from the venerable Chief Justice of the Supreme Court.*

"After the ceremony of inauguration had been completed, the President and Ex-President retired by the same avenue, and the procession, or the military part of it, marched to the executive mansion. On arriving at the President's house, Mr. Lincoln met Gen. Scott, by whom he was warmly greeted; and then the doors of the house were opened, and thousands of persons rapidly passed through, shaking hands with the President, who stood in the reception-room for that purpose. In this simple and quiet manner was a change of rulers made." †

* Chief Justice Taney administered this oath to ten successive presidents.

† "Annual Cyclopædia," 1861.

And thus the lowly-born son of the Western pioneer sat down in the presidential chair of a great Republic, — a seat more honorable than any throne on earth. The contrast between his humble home in early life and this

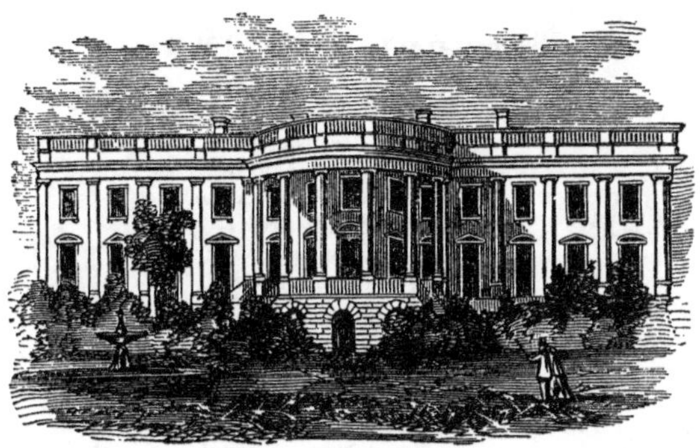

WHITE HOUSE, D. C.

high position is seen in the sketch thus purposely given of the imposing ceremonies of inauguration. Well might the eloquent statesman* add, after mentioning Cæsar, William of Orange, and Henry IV. of France, all of whom were assassinated, "his star will not pale by the side of theirs. . . . These are illustrious names; but there is nothing in them which can eclipse the simple life of our President, whose example will be an epoch in the history of humanity, and a rebuke to every usurper, to be commemorated forever by history and by song. 'I called thee from the sheep-cot to be ruler over Israel,' said the Lord to David; and whoever is thus called is more than Cæsar. Such an appointment was his; and his simple devotion to human rights was more than genius or power."

* Hon. Charles Sumner.

CHAPTER V.

TROUBLOUS TIMES.

> **"We wait beneath the furnace-blast**
> **The pangs of transformation:**
> **Not painlessly doth God recast**
> **And mould anew the nation.**
> **Hot burns the fire**
> **Where wrongs expire;**
> **Nor spares the hand**
> **That from the land**
> **Uproots the ancient evil."**
>
> **WHITTIER.**

> **"I am for peace; but, when I speak, they are for war." — Ps. cxx. 7.**

THE "Quaker drop" showed itself in the inaugural address of the new President. The blood of a pious and peaceful ancestry coursed along the veins of him whom God had called to be the head of a great nation in its most troublous times: with a prescience belonging to that inheritance, he saw the gathering cloud, and heard the thunders of war. Yet he would fain stay the glittering bolt of destiny, and, if possible, forbid the clashing of contending steel. Hence the deprecatory tone of his first inaugural; the evident desire for peace, that shone, like the golden symbol of the descending Spirit, in the illuminated missals of other days. But it was unavailing. The soft utterances of peace were drowned in the noisy clamors of war; and the closing paragraph of that inaugural address was, even more than its author knew, the very voice of prophecy. Only a few short months, and "the mystic cords of memory" did stretch from many a "battle-field and patriot grave" to living hearts and hearth-stones all over our broad land; and at the close of the mighty conflict, from his own grave — the grave of a martyr — was to come a voice pleading with humanity for liberty and righteousness. But we will not anticipate.

Mr. Lincoln's first act was to choose a Cabinet. This he did with his usual discrimination; and though the lapse of time and changing course of events led to changes in the Cabinet, yet none are willing to impeach the wisdom which selected the first set of Cabinet-officers. For the important position of Secretary of State, William H. Seward of New York was selected; Salmon P. Chase of Ohio was placed in charge of the Treasury Department; Simon Cameron of Pennsylvania became Secretary of War; Gideon Welles of Connecticut, Secretary of the Navy; Caleb B. Smith of Indiana, Secretary of the Interior; Montgomery Blair of Maryland was appointed Postmaster-General; and Edward Bates of Missouri, Attorney-General.

As every reader of to-day knows, the Southern States manifested a rebellious spirit long before Lincoln filled the chair of Washington. Had the imbecile Buchanan but possessed the old Roman spirit of one of his predecessors, he would have shown that he had a "backbone," and taken a Jacksonian share of the "responsibility" in using measures that would have crushed the viper in the egg. But the pusillanimous policy adopted just suited the "let-me-alone" theory of the Southern secessionists; and so the infamous Floyd could steal our arms, and the double-dyed traitor, Robert E. Lee, could linger in our ranks till he had possessed himself of Gen. Scott's plans, and then desert to the enemy, thenceforth to use his knowledge in an effort to overthrow the best Government the world ever saw, and place a man, who disgraced the name of a former President of our Republic, on a throne, the corner-stone of whose tottering pedestal was human slavery. And thus Buchanan made the way rough and hard for Lincoln. But the hour and the man were ready for each other. The President went calmly forward. "Coming to the presidency pre-occupied by the traditional theories and opinions of the political school in which he was educated, he devoted himself with a purpose single and exclusive to the practical interpretation of events, to the study of those lessons taught by the experience through which the country was called to pass; and learning, in common with a majority of his countrymen, in the strifes and agonies of the Rebellion, by the lurid glare of the fires of treason and of civil war, how to accommodate opinion to the altered relations of States, interests, and sections of the people, he marched, side by side with the advancing hosts of the best and most discerning, in the direction where Divine Providence pointed the way." *

Yet he could not conscientiously counsel war at first. His inaugural was an olive-branch vainly held out to hands that would not receive it. Then came a pause after its utterance. It was the lull before the storm; the portentous calm that precedes the burst of the tornado. "Since the close of the Revolutionary struggle, no man had seen in the free States any other banner floating over a regiment of our people than the stars and stripes: though the waves of party-spirit had often run mountain-high, and we had seemed just on the brink of disruption and civil war, yet the dreaded collision had always been somehow averted, and the moment of fiercest excitement, of wildest alienation, had often been the im-

* Gov. Andrew's Address.

mediate precursor of a halcyon era of reconciliation, peace, and fraternal harmony. It was not easy for Northern men, especially those who never visited and sojourned at the South, to comprehend and realize the wide prevalence and intensity of anti-national sentiment and feeling in those localities whose social order, industry and business, were entirely based on slavery. Neither envying nor hating the Southerners while lamenting their delusions and restricting their exactions, it was hard indeed for many, if not most, of the citizens of the free States to realize that we stood on the brink of a volcano whose rumbling precluded an eruption of blood as well as ashes." *

But the country seemed unprepared for war in every sense. Jefferson Davis and John B. Floyd had directed the War Department for eight years with an eye to Southern supremacy. Most of our little army had been ordered to Texas, where it was placed under command of the rebel general Twiggs, who soon betrayed it into the hands of his fellow-traitors. Floyd had acted the part of a thief in transferring arms and ammunition from Northern to Southern arsenals; and the larger and better portion of our little navy had been scattered over distant seas. Now, the South desired to gain entire possession of the forts along her shores, and thus obtain means to defy the North when it would collect the revenue that it should receive from vessels entering Southern ports. This, President Lincoln could not allow.

Yet he was slow to declare war. He could not, until it seemed unavoidable, imbrue his hands in a brother's blood. Hear his own words in reference to the Mexican War, spoken while a member of Congress: "Now, sir,

* Greeley's "History of the American Conflict," p. 429.

for the purpose of obtaining the very best evidence as to whether Texas had actually carried her revolution to the place where the hostilities of the present war commenced, let the President answer the interrogations I proposed. Let him answer fully, fairly, and candidly. Let him answer with *facts*, not with arguments. Let him remember he sits where Washington sat; and, so remembering, let him answer as Washington would answer. As a nation *should* not, and the Almighty *will* not, be evaded, so let him attempt no evasion, no equivocation. . . . But if he cannot or will not do this; if, on any pretence or no pretence, he shall refuse or omit it, — then I shall be fully convinced of what I more than suspect already, — that he is deeply conscious of being in the wrong; that he feels the blood of this war, like the blood of Abel, is crying to heaven against him; that he ordered Gen. Taylor into the midst of a peaceful Mexican settlement purposely to bring on a war; . . . and, trusting to escape scrutiny by fixing the public gaze upon the exceeding brightness of military glory, — that attractive rainbow that rises in showers of blood, that serpent's eye that charms to destroy, — he plunged into it, and has swept on and on, till, disappointed in his calculation of the ease with which Mexico might be subdued, he now finds himself he knows not where." *

Now Lincoln himself sat where the great man he venerated once sat; and he felt that it became him to think calmly and soberly, and to act only after the severest scrutiny and profoundest deliberation, and, above all, not till the leadings of Divine Providence had shown him the path of duty. He had no wish to emulate Napoleon or Alexander; no desire to be a second Cain. Not a gleam

* "President's Words," p. 20.

of military glory dazzled his peace-loving eyes, nor did any murderous purpose lurk in his soul; and, when he finally came to the conclusion that war was inevitable, it was with a sadness like that which must have wrapped the brow of Abraham in gloom ere he offered up his beloved Isaac; or like that which deepened the lines of sorrow and bade the tears glisten on His face who bowed himself over Jerusalem, mourning the desolation that must come upon her for her disobedience.

Lincoln was no party-man; or, if he ever had been, the exigencies of the times, or rather the providence of God, which was preparing him for those times, bade him rise above mere party-limits.

When he had borne the heavy burdens of two war-cursed years, his language was that of a wisdom which showed a discrimination based on integrity of purpose. Said he in May, 1863, with characteristic plainness and accuracy of speech, "The dissensions between Union men in Missouri are due solely to a factious spirit which is exceedingly reprehensible. The two parties ought to have their heads knocked together. Either would rather see the defeat of their adversary than that of Jefferson Davis. We are in civil war. In such cases, there is always a main question; but, in this case, that question is a perplexing compound,— union and slavery. It becomes a question not of two sides merely, but of at least four sides, even among those who are for the Union, saying nothing of those who are against it: thus those who are for the Union *with*, but *not without*, slavery; those for it *without*, but not *with;* those for it *with* or *without*, but prefer it *with;* and those for it *with* or *without*, but prefer it *without.*"

And, with a wisdom which could only have come from

above, Lincoln guided the Ship of State month after month, year after after year, carefully avoiding Scylla on the one hand, and Charybdis on the other. Men could not always see this; and more than one sought for a life-preserver, deeming shipwreck inevitable. But though the wild waters heaved tumultuously, and the huge breakers lifted their crested heads, and filled the ear of every listener with their tremendous voice, "deep calling unto deep" in the hour of our nation's dismay, yet calmly and steadily the hand of God's appointed pilot grasped the helm; and the eye of Abraham Lincoln glanced only from the needle that indicated the path of justice, to the star that rose in the East, and heralded the day of freedom.

The parricidal hands of Southern traitors were at last raised against their father-land; and at "3.20, A.M., of the 12th of April, 1861, Major Anderson was duly notified that fire would be opened on Fort Sumter in one hour. Punctual to the appointed moment, the roar of a mortar from Sullivan's Island, quickly followed by the rustling shriek of a shell, gave notice to the world that the era of compromise and diplomacy was ended; that the slaveholders' confederacy had appealed from sterile negotiations to the 'last argument' of aristocracies as well as kings. Another gun from that island quickly repeated the warning, waking a response from battery after battery, until Sumter appeared the focus of a circle of volcanic fire. Soon the thunder of fifty heavy breaching-cannon, in one grand volley, followed by the crashing and crumbling of brick, stone, and mortar around and above them, apprised the little garrison that their stay in those quarters must necessarily be short." *

And reluctantly the brave defenders of the star-

* Greeley's "History."

spangled banner were compelled to surrender. We all know the story of Fort Sumter. Every loyal heart acknowledged Major Anderson a hero and a patriot; and when, on Monday morning, April 15, 1861, President Lincoln issued his first proclamation,* calling for the country's defenders, there came a universal "Amen" to the call.

"'COME TO THE RESCUE!' The cry went forth
Through the length and breadth of the loyal North;
For the gun that startled Sumter heard
Wakened the land with its fiery word.
The farmer paused with his work half done,
And snatched from the nail his rusty gun;
And the swart mechanic wiped his brow,
Shouting, 'There's work for my strong arm now!'
And the parson doffed his gown, and said,
'Bring me my right good sword instead;'
And the scholar paused in his eager quest,
And buckled his belt on with the rest;
And each and all to the rescue went
As unto a royal tournament:
For the loyal blood of a nation stirred
To the gun that startled Sumter heard." †

Governors and legislatures vied with each other in proffers of men and money to the Government. The Governor of Rhode Island, who was not a Republican, not only promptly raised the quota of men required, but actually led it to Washington and to the battle-field. The same feeling of self-sacrificing patriotism nerved the heart and arm of privates as well as officers. "Among the privates in Rhode Island's first regiment was one worth a million dollars, who destroyed the passage-ticket he had bought for a voyage to Europe on a tour of ob-

* See Chapter VIII.

† Mrs. Caroline A. Mason.

servation and pleasure, to shoulder his musket in defence of his country and her laws." *

On marched the loyal soldiers of New England to defend the Capitol of their country. As Gov. Andrew said to the Mayor of Baltimore, "Their march through New York was triumphal." But "bloody Baltimore" chose to re-enact the scenes of the 19th of April, 1778; and on the 19th of April, 1861, —

"The streets our soldier-fathers trod
Blushed with their children's gore:
We saw the craven rulers nod,
And dip in blood the civic rod.
Shall such things be, O righteous God!
In Baltimore?" †

The blood of Massachusetts patriots crimsoned the stones of Baltimore; ‡ and as the news came back to the New-England States, it was as if the "fiery cross" had been lighted, and passed from hand to hand, calling anew to battle the clans of freemen who were ready to rally for liberty and law.

Gen. Butler (Cœur de Lion), with the dauntless Eighth Massachusetts, ably seconded by the New-York Seventh, followed in the sanguinary wake of the Sixth

* Greeley's "History," &c. † Bayard Taylor.

‡ Their death called forth the historic telegram from Gov. Andrew to Mayor Brown: "I pray you to cause the bodies of our Massachusetts soldiers, dead in Baltimore, to be laid out, preserved in ice, and tenderly sent forward by express to me. All expenses will be paid by the Commonwealth." Their early martyrdom in the dear cause of Liberty unsheathed many a sword that else had remained in its scabbard, and awoke the music of many a poet's lyre. Said one (Mary Webb), with prophetic utterance, —

"Peace to their ashes! they sleep well, —
Our Massachusetts dead, who fell
In march to Freedom's citadel;
First-fruits of that full vintage red,
Awaiting War's all-crushing tread;
Our own, our Massachusetts dead!"

Massachusetts, whose blood, as in the days of Revolutionary struggle, was the first to be shed for liberty; and soon the Capitol was in safety from the threatening parricides of the South.*

But the first blood was not the last; and the pride of New-England homes was mown down upon many a battle-field, as we all know too well, during these troublous times. Ellsworth and Lyon and Baker were early laid in patriot-graves. Bull Run, Ball's Bluff, Antietam, Fredericksburg, Gettysburg, and many a battle-field besides, call up the memories of the loved and lost, who bravely gave their lives for their country: we think of gallant Dix who died exclaiming, "The Iowa Third never surrenders!" of the brave young captain Derby, who led his men undauntedly, till he —

"By the wayside fell and perished;"

of the heroic chaplain Fuller, who felt that he "must do something for his country," and shouldered a musket in her defence: we think of many, many brave, true hearts that throb no more on earth, — all fallen victims to the relentless war which has scourged our nation into a repentance of its vilest sin; and we feel as if President Lincoln needed to have "the spirit of wisdom, and counsel, and of ghostly strength" given to him, almost "without measure," that he might know how to deal with the various problems which came up to be solved by him. Gen. Butler aided to solve one, when he pronounced the slaves of the rebels "contraband of war."

Our arms knew victory, and knew also disaster. It

* While our country had a Judas in the person of every rebel chief, it was not without its Peter. "An officer who called at the White House during the dark days when Washington was isolated, and threatened from every side, and said to Mr. Lincoln, 'Every one else may desert you, but I never will,' two days after absconded, and became afterward a Confederate major-general."

was doubtless well that we had some reverses, or we should have been too confident, and less careful about purging the nation from its gross iniquity. Slowly the wheels of time rolled on; and as slowly, but as surely also, travelled the President in his ideas of what was his duty and that of the nation. Some thought him an "old fogy;" some were ready to label him as a fossil, and put him on the shelf. One sneeringly said he was "not to be blamed for incapacity;" but, unmoved by slights or frowns or jeers, the man of the people sought to benefit the people, and do the work that God had given him to do. Mistakes he might make, for he was human; but none that were irretrievable. Mordecai asked Esther, "Who knoweth whether thou art come to the kingdom for such a time as this?" And the same might have been asked of our late President, sure that the answer would indicate a willingness to "spend and be spent" in the discharge of duty.

CHAPTER VI.

THE COURSE PURSUED.

"Stand by the flag, all doubt and treason scorning:
Believe, with courage firm and faith sublime,
That it will float until the Eternal Morning
Pales with its glories all the lights of Time."

"The Spirit of the Lord God is upon me, because the Lord hath anointed me to preach good tidings unto the meek: he hath sent me to bind up the broken-hearted, to proclaim liberty to the captives, and the opening of the prison to them that are bound." — ISA. lxi. 1.

THE years went on. Once more our nation knew by bitter personal experience the meaning of the phrase, — "Times that tried men's souls." President Lincoln marched abreast of the times, perhaps, not infrequently, cautious about being far in advance.

This volume is not intended to be a history of the war, or even a record of all the acts of the President in regard to the war; for then it must exceed the designed limits: but it may give brief hints of the course pursued; not a panorama of the whole path, but stereoscopic views, it may be, here and there.

It was no easy thing to conduct the civil war which was inaugurated in 1861 to its triumphal close in 1865. But God was alike with the nation which was in the caldron, and the man who, in one sense, bore the burden of that nation's woes.

As Bancroft, our great historian, has said, after referring to the uprising of the loyal North, "In some respects Abraham Lincoln was peculiarly fitted for his task, in connection with the movement of his countrymen.

He was of the North-west; and this time it was the Mississippi River, the needed outlet for the wealth of the North-west, that did its part in asserting the necessity of the Union. He was one of the mass of the people; he represented them because he was of them; and the mass of the people, the class that lives and thrives by self-imposed labor, felt that the work which was to be done was a work of their own,—the assertion of equality against the pride of oligarchy; of free labor against the lordship over slaves; of the great industrial people against all the expiring aristocracies of which any remnants had tided down from the middle ages. He was of a religious turn of mind, without superstition; and the unbroken faith of the mass was like his own. As he went along through his difficult journey, sounding his way, he held fast by the hand of the people, and 'tracked his footsteps with even feet.' 'His pulse's beat twined with their pulses.' "*

The war was, as we have said, a *necessity*, which the President accepted because he could not do otherwise. It was "majestic, resistless, as when God flings out the banner of the storm, and bids it move. It swept on. No man guided it, no man could foretell its duration or its issues. So tumultuous and perplexed were the movements, that the avowed and wise policy of the President was to have no policy, but simply an end sought as wisdom might be given moment by moment. It came to this, that all that men knew was that there was nothing to do but to fight on. And they did fight. And oh the agony of those days! 'We waited for light, but, behold, obscurity; for brightness, but we walked in darkness.' We cried out, 'O thou sword of the Lord! how

* "Atlantic Monthly," June, 1865.

long will it be ere thou be quiet? Put thyself up into thy scabbard; rest, and be still.' But the voice came, 'How can it be quiet, seeing the Lord hath given it a charge?' And what that charge was, those who watched began, after a time, to discover. It was first to lift the negro up into manhood by bringing him into line with the white man in fighting the battles of freedom. We all know how this was resisted and scoffed at. It could not be. But the pressure did not lift; it waxed heavier and heavier; and it was done. The negro fought and was welcomed. A second charge was to make the Proclamation of Emancipation, ridiculed as the Pope's bull against the comet, to make that as the breath of the Almighty to sweep away slavery. That was done. Again the charge was to bring the South, the chivalry, to recognize by public act the manhood of the negro by making him a soldier, and by confessing the dependence of their cause upon him. This was all: it was enough. When this was done, the war ceased." *

The course pursued by the President was just such as to secure the results above mentioned. He was emphatically the "right man in the right place." Gov. Andrew has so well described the man and his course in regard to the affairs of the nation, that no other words seem needed. He says of the President, "He had the rare gift of discerning and setting aside whatever is extraneous and accidental, and of simplifying an inquiry or an argument by just discriminations. The purpose of his mind waited for the instruction of his deliberate judgment; and he was never ashamed to hesitate until he was sure it was intelligently formed. Not greatly gifted in what is called the intuition of reason, he was, never-

* Rev. Mark Hopkins, D.D., President of Williams College, in a sermon on "Providence and Revelation," before the graduating class of 1865.

theless, of so honest an intellect, that, by the processes of methodical reasoning, he was often led so directly to his result, that he occasionally seemed to rise into that peculiar sphere which we assign to those who by original constitution are natural leaders among men. Not by nature a leader, neither was he by nature a follower; and by force of his rare union and balance of certain qualities, both intellectual and moral, he was enabled to rise to the dignity of master of his own position in a place exacting and difficult almost beyond the precedents of history. Educated wholly as a civilian, his fame will be forever associated with his administration of public affairs in a civil war, unexampled in its proportions, and conducted on his own side with such success as to command his own re-election by the free will of a free people. . . . Possessed of a will of unusual firmness and tenacity, his heart was placable, humane, and tender. He exerted powers the most extensive and various, stretching into that undefined and dangerous region of administrative jurisprudence, where the rights and duties of military commander-in-chief limit and merge into themselves the functions of the civil magistrate, and even of the judicial tribunal. And yet, if we should concede to his enemies all that disappointed animosity and defeated disloyalty have been able to allege against him, we should still be able to challenge all human history to produce the name of a ruler more just, unselfish, or unresentful. Cheerful, patient, and without egotism, he regarded and treated himself as the servant of the people, using his powers only for their cause; using no more than the cause seemed clearly to demand, and using them alike without passion and without perturbation.

"It were premature for us to assert how, or how far,

during the four years of his administration, he *led* the American people. The unfolding of events in the history we are yet to enact will alone determine the limits of such influence. It is enough for his immortal glory that he faithfully *represented* this people, their confidence in democratic government, their constancy in the hour of adversity, and their magnanimity in the hour of triumph."

Yet whether fully acknowledged as a leader by all, or not, Abraham Lincoln was truly great, and his course one of profoundest wisdom. He was "great in clearness of thought, great in calm deliberation, great in earnestness, in unaffectedness, in unselfish devotion to duty. . . .

"Raised moderately to the station which Washington was the first to fill, his sudden elevation sent a pang to the hearts of many, as though a sad degeneracy had fallen on our times; while others shuddered at the unequalness of the man for the most critical position which had yet arisen in American affairs.

"Four years have so changed all this, that his name is universally revered; the great qualities which he really possessed, his knowledge of men, his uprightness and honesty, his kindness of heart, his extreme caution in the unnumbered difficulties that daily arose in the constant civil and military emergencies, with a firmness that was never swerved by flattery or fear,—all these, and the great results effected under his administration, have given him in the heart of the people a place second only to that of the father of his country." *

Not always did the President find a hearty co-operation in his plans, or a rightful appreciation of his course. We can see the straightforward, positive, yet peaceful

* "Lincoln Memorial."

character of the man in his words to some such cavillers. Said he, in August, 1863, —

"To those who are dissatisfied with me, I would say, You desired peace, and you blame me that we do not have it. But how can we attain it? There are but three conceivable ways. First, to suppress the Rebellion by force of arms. This I am trying to do. Are you for it? If you are, so far we are agreed. If you are not for it, a second way is to give up the Union. I am against this. Are you for it? If you are, you should say so plainly. If you are not for force, nor yet for dissolution, there only remains some imaginable compromise."

And as to compromise, he could only say, "I do not believe that any compromise, embracing the maintenance of the Union, is now possible. All that I learn tends to a directly opposite belief. The strength of the Rebellion is its military,—its army. In any compromise, we should waste time, which the enemy would improve to our disadvantage; and that would be all."

Again: in reference to his course, he uttered, not an apology, but words of manly defence, saying, in April, 1864, "Was it possible to lose the nation, and yet preserve the Constitution? By general law, life *and* limb must be protected: yet often a *limb* must be amputated to save a life; but a *life* is never wisely given to save a *limb*. I felt that measures otherwise unconstitutional might become lawful by becoming indispensable to the preservation of the nation. Right or wrong, I assumed this ground, and now avow it. I could not feel, that, to the best of my ability, I had ever tried to preserve the Constitution, if, to save slavery or any minor matter, I should permit the wreck of Government, Country, and Constitution altogether."

It was not his party, it was not himself, but it was *his*

country, for which he labored. The course he pursued while President had only the good of the united whole in view. Hence, on one occasion, he advised that all *work together* for the nation's good, in these words: —

"Let the nation take hold of the larger works, and the States the smaller ones; and thus, working in a meeting direction, discreetly, but steadily and firmly, what is made unequal in one place may be equalized in another, extravagance avoided, and the whole country put on that career of prosperity which shall correspond with its extent of territory, its natural resources, and the intelligence and enterprise of its people."

Hear the words of the senator whose personal wounds from the minions of slavery give him the right to be known as Liberty's champion. What says he of Abraham Lincoln in the troublous times, and of the course he pursued? This: —

"He was placed by Providence at the head of his country during an unprecedented crisis, when the fountains of the great deep were broken up, and men turned for protection to military power. Multitudinous armies were mustered. Great navies were set on foot. Of all these he was the constitutional commander-in-chief. As the war proceeded, all his prerogatives enlarged, and others sprang into being, until the sway of a Republican President became imperatorial and imperial. But not for one moment did the modesty of his nature desert him. His constant thought was his country, and how to serve it. Personal ambition at the expense of patriotism was as far removed from the simple purity of his nature as poison from a strawberry. And thus with equal courage in the darkest hour he continued on, heeding as little the warnings of danger as the temptations of power. 'It would not do for a President,' he said, 'to have guards with drawn sabres at his door, as if he fancied he were, or were trying to be, or were assuming to be, an emperor.' And in the same simplicity, he spoke of his return at morning to his daily duties as 'opening shop.'

"When he became President, he was without any considerable experience in public affairs; nor was he much versed in history, whose lessons would have been most valuable. As he became more familiar with the place, his facility evidently increased. He had 'learned the ropes,' so he said. But his habits of business were irregular, and they were never those of despatch. He did not see at once the just proportions of things, and allowed himself to be too much occupied by details. Even in small things, as well as in great, there was in him a certain resistance to be overcome. There were moments when this delay caused impatience, and important questions seemed to suffer. But, when the blow was struck, there was nothing but gratitude; and all confessed the singleness with which he had sought the public good. There was also a conviction, that, though slow to reach his conclusion, he was inflexible in maintaining it. Pompey boasted that by the stamp of his foot he might raise an army. The President might have done the same; but, according to his own words, he 'put his foot down,' and saved a principle."

Let it be remembered evermore that the course of events beyond his control, and the course he pursued when the power was in his hands for a season, both culminated in the triumph of freedom in our liberty-boasting land. In a letter dated April 4, 1864, President Lincoln declared, "If slavery is not wrong, nothing is wrong;" and as an English divine has well said,—

"This wrong of slavery, he, more than any other man of our day, has been instrumental in removing. It was his well-known hostility to it, which, on his election, was the proximate and avowed cause of the Rebellion. As far as his pledges to the law and the course of events permitted, he steadily pursued this great object. Under his auspices, slavery was speedly abolished in Columbia, and prohibited in the Territories. The slave-trade was declared penal, and the right of search fully granted. The loyal States were invited to emancipate their slaves, full compensation being offered. Then the proclamation was issued by which all slaves in rebel States were declared free; and though, for a season, this was inoperative over a large district, it is now not only law, but fact. During the war, two millions of slaves actually gained their freedom, and were protected wherever the power of the President extended. And now throughout those Southern States, long a house of cruel bondage, the jubilee trumpet is sounding deliverance to the captive, and the opening of the prison to them that are bound."

The President was not only nominally the commander-in-chief of the Union forces, but he assumed active command, and gave evidence of his independence and fearlessness in the discharge of duty by promulgating three important military orders, — ordering a general and combined movement of the forces on land and sea, requiring that the Army of the Potomac be organized into corps; confining Gen. McClellan to the command of the Department of the Potomac; and organizing the Department of the Mississippi and the Mountain Department.

This was in March, 1862. On the 19th of the previous month, he had issued a proclamation requesting the people of the United States to assemble on the anniversary of Washington's birth, and celebrate the day by reading the memorable "Farewell Address." This was done in almost every town and city of the loyal States.

In July, 1862, the President conferred with the loyal governors, and yielded to their desire that more men should be summoned to the defence of the country. The senators and representatives of the border States were at this time invited to a personal conference; and the President talked freely with them in regard to gradual emancipation, reading to them a letter which he had prepared, in which he stated his views explicitly, and closed it with the following eloquent appeal: "You are patriots and statesmen; and, as such, I pray you consider this proposition, and, at the least, commend it to the consideration of your States and people. As you would perpetuate popular government for the best people in the world, I beseech you that you do in no wise omit this. Our common country is in great peril, demanding the loftiest views and boldest action to bring a speedy relief. Once relieved, its form of government is saved to the world, its beloved history and cherished memories are vindicated, and its happy future fully assured, and rendered inconceivably grand. To you, more than to any others, the privilege is given to assure that happiness and swell that grandeur, and to link your own names therewith forever."

An able article in the leading Review* of our land expatiates upon the progress of the country towards an acknowledgment of freedom and equality for all, without distinction of color, and says, —

"While every day was bringing the people nearer to the conclusion which all thinking men saw to be inevitable from the beginning, it was wise in Mr. Lincoln to leave the shaping of his policy to events. In this country, where the rough and ready understanding of the

* "North-American Review" for January, 1864.

people is sure at last to be the controlling power, a profound common sense is the best genius for statemanship. Hitherto the wisdom of the President's measures has been justified by the fact that they have always resulted in more firmly uniting public opinion."

It is manifestly evident to candid minds that slavery was the cause of our troublous times, and that the course pursued by the President, under divine direction, was such as to overthrow slavery, and thus secure peace. There could be no permanent peace or prosperity with that accursed system among us, which the great Methodist, John Wesley, declared to be "the sum of all villanies."

President Hopkins, of Williams College, has summed up the proofs of the direful effects of slavery in the following words: —

"Slavery may stand as the type and culmination of all oppressive systems, and the testimony consists in a manifestation of its legitimate and matured fruits.

"Till our armies went South, and Southern prisoners came North, there was but a slight impression among us of the general ignorance under such a system; of the number who could not read, or sign their names. But for this ignorance, there could have been no rebellion. There had been no adequate conception of the want of thrift and general behind-handedness, nor of the pervading spirit at once of license and of despotism. What were called the abuses of the system were more frequent and foul than had been supposed. But these are little compared with the spirit of the system as revealed, — first by atrocities in the treatment of Southern Union men, not exceeded by any thing in the Sepoy Rebellion; second by the massacre at Fort Pillow, intended to be the inauguration of a policy; third by the preparations to blow up Libby Prison; fourth by the deliberate, systematic, long-continued exposure, neglect, and starvation of Union prisoners; and, finally, by the assassination of the President. These things we do not charge to all the people of the South. They are like other men. Many are better than their system: but we do charge them to the spirit of the system; and we say, that by these exposures and revelations, culminating as they did in a way to send a thrill of horror through the civilized world, God has pilloried the system before the nations, and all that has affinity with it.

"That there were atrocities on our side we do not deny. They are incident to war. But we do deny any thing that can be at all an offset to such a record. It is to be said further on the part of the North, that the war was carried on here chiefly without proscription; and that, in connection with it, there were the Sanitary and Christian Commissions that furnished by voluntary contribution millions for the aid of wounded and sick soldiers, to be applied equally, so far as might be, to friend and foe. Any thing like these, in connection with war, no institutions or form of government had ever before developed."

We of the North could not, then, be accused of barbarism further than war necessarily involves. We fought under a commander-in-chief whose heart was as tender as a father toward his soldiers, and who was as lenient towards his enemies as He could desire who said, "Bless them that curse you." But he was a magistrate, and it was not for him to "bear the sword in vain."

God knew the heart of our beloved Lincoln; and He, who prepared him for the glorious work before him, undoubtedly approved of the course he pursued while the country of his patriot love was writhing like a second Laocoön in the terrible folds of the serpent Treason.

CHAPTER VII.

PECULIAR TRIALS.

"Trials make the promise sweet,
Trials give new life to prayer,
Bring me to my Saviour's feet,
Lay me low, and keep me there."

"These are they that came up out of great tribulation, and have washed their robes, and made them white in the blood of the Lamb." — REV. vii. 14.

ALL great and noble natures have their great and peculiar trials; and no name stands on the heights of history, as a beacon for the nations, which has not been fitted for its position by trial and suffering. One far-seeing woman of our land has said, "Whatever is highest and holiest is tinged with melancholy. The eye of genius has always a plaintive expression, and its natural language is pathos. A prophet is sadder than other men; and He who was greater than all prophets was a man of sorrows, and acquainted with grief." * And another, whose own experience has taught her the taste of Marah's waters, and whose "Uncle Tom" was the creature of her sympathy with sorrow, as well as the truthful exponent of the woes of slavery, has said, with the force of highest wisdom, "Sorrow is the great birth-agony of immortal powers; sorrow is the great searcher and revealer of hearts, the great test of truth; . . . sorrow reveals forces in ourselves of which we never dreamed; . . . sorrow is divine. Sorrow is reigning on

* Mrs. Lydia Maria Child.

the throne of the universe, and the crown of all crowns has been one of thorns." *

It is evident that the ministry of sorrow to the human soul is one which elevates, strengthens, purifies. It is among the "all things" that "work together for good" to the child of God. Abraham Lincoln was among those favored ones for whom the "light afflictions" of this world were to "work the far more exceeding and eternal weight of glory." Of some peculiar trials which his great soul experienced during the years of his presidency, it is here designed to speak; though it may be true that other weights were upon his expanding spirit, and other trials, even more grievous, oppressed his soul: for, evermore, the hidden sorrow is deepest, and only the human heart itself knoweth its own bitterness. By the very greatness of Lincoln's character, we may measure the discipline of trial and sorrow through which he had to pass while a sojourner on earth. This life is the childhood of our existence; and God deals with us all as a father with his children, wisely correcting us in needed discipline, for our highest good.

We know some of the trials of his early life, his bitter grief at the loss of a beloved mother, his struggles amid poverty and other discouragements. And, when he became the President of the vast Republic, there was laid upon him the burden of responsibility which must rest upon a leader in the time of civil war.

His personal friend Col. Deming declares, "The hour when doubt and hesitancy first yielded to the stern command of remorseless duty must have been the soberest, saddest, solemnest of his faithful life, not from doubt of the result, though that was sufficiently perplexing; not

* Mrs. Stowe's "Minister's Wooing."

from fear of the consequences, though these were appalling enough; not from the weight of responsibility, though that might have staggered the most unyielding determination; but it was sad and solemn, because Abraham Lincoln above and beyond all other men loved peace, and hated war; because sieges, battles, strife, swords, bayoets, rifles, cannon, all the paraphernalia and instruments of brute force, were abhorrent to his enlightened and benevolent nature. Shall we raise the latch, and enter into the secret chamber of that capacious and genial soul when this fell resolve was first reached; when the frightful vision of war, in all its terrors clad, supplants there the hope of conciliation and the dream of peace? I speak what I heard from his own lips, when I say, that it was reached after sleepless nights, after a severe conflict with himself, and with extreme reluctance. By a strange and cruel freak of fate, the duty of waging the bloodiest war in history was imposed upon the most peace-loving and amiable ruler in all time; upon a man whose maxim was, in the language of one of his favorite texts, 'Let the potsherd strive with the potsherds of the earth;' and into whose mind had been thoroughly ingrained that traditional notion of our politics, — that the first drop of blood shed in a sectional strife was the death-knell of the American Union.

"Let us enter in where that now disembodied spirit was, in the recesses of its clay tenement, in stormy debate with itself. What throes, what agony, do we witness! — what heart-rending sobs, what heaven-piercing prayers, that the cup may pass from his lips! Here was that conservative mind, trained to habits of professional caution, with the strongest bias towards legality and moderation, which had uniformly steered itself by the certain lights of jurisprudence; which had invoked no remedies but the peaceful ones of the courts, the Constitution, and the law; which had never combated error but with reason and persuasion alone, and had abjured the ordeal of battle, and the arbitrament of force, as absolute and heathenish enormities, — here are all these mature, earnest opinions, and prepossessions, all dominant from fifty years of independent sway, wrestling impotently with the war ideas, and the overmastering war revelation, of yesterday. What an unwelcome intruder the conviction is to the serene virtues, which had hitherto exclusively occupied this holy sanctuary! Domesticated here are Justice and Mercy (and 'earthly power is likest God's when Mercy seasons Justice'),—Justice and Mercy, which hold the balances quite evenly, but the hair's weight which oscillates them uniformly found in Mercy's scale; and how repulsive it is to these righteous and discriminating attributes to let loose upon the people a wild and furious avenger that devours alike innocence and guilt!

"Here, too, dwell sensibilities and affections so acute, that they fling wide open the doors of the soul to every one who approaches in misfortune's name, grant the prayer of sorrow before it is half uttered, and which the inarticulate wail of infancy instantly melts into tears of most compassionate tenderness. How are these sensitive fibres wrung and tortured when it suddenly flashes upon them that the loving hand, which has learned only to soothe and relieve the miserable, is commissioned by inexorable fate to break the fourth seal of the Apocalypse, and, 'behold, a pale horse! and his name who sat on him was Death, and Hell followed him; and power was given unto them over the fourth part of the earth to kill with the sword and with hunger and with death, and with the beasts of the earth.'

"Movelessly, movelessly rooted also in this great heart is a superfine sense of humor, craving hilarity and harmless mirth, and joy-inspiring wit and anecdote, as the only effectual relief to an over-anxious spirit and an overtaxed brain; and how reluctantly does this part of his nature admit to close companionship the gloomy forebodings, the little memories, the dreadful uncertainties, the everlasting shrieks, dirges, vengeful tragedies, and heart-rending atrocities, of war!"

This vivid portrayal of Lincoln's character and feelings shows us one of his peculiar trials. He suffered during the struggle which preceded his decision that the war must be prosecuted; and he suffered during its continuance by the constant jarring of the machinery he was seeking to keep in motion. His motives were misunderstood, his character maligned, and his plans often frustrated, by those whose best good he was continually studying.

In common with his loyal countrymen, he felt the gloom of those hours of the war when defeat lowered our beautiful banner; but he felt it with peculiar force because he was the leader. "How nobly the President bore himself during this interval of darkness that could be felt, when bold men trembled at every click of the telegraph, let two tributes, offered by unfriendly voices to his stoicism, attest: the first is from no less a master of it than Napoleon the Third, who epigrammatically says, 'Mr. Lincoln's highest claim upon my admiration is a Roman equanimity, which has been tried by both extremes of fortune, and disturbed by neither.' The second is from a hostile Englishman, who says, that, 'tried by years of failure, without achieving one great success, he not only never yielded to despondency or anger, but, what is most marvellous, continually grew in self-possession and magnaminity.'

"I once myself ventured to ask the President if he had ever despaired of the country; and he told me, that, when the Peninsular campaign terminated suddenly at Harrison's Landing, he was as nearly inconsolable as he could be, and live. In the same connection, I inquired if there had ever been a period in which he thought that better management upon the part of his commanding-general might have terminated the war: and he answered that there were three; that the first was at Malvern Hill, when McClellan failed to command an immediate advance upon Richmond; that the second was at Chancellorville, where Hooker failed to re-enforce Sedgwick after hearing his cannon upon the extreme right; and that the third was after Lee's retreat from Gettysburg, when Meade failed to attack him in the bend of the Potomac. After this commentary, I waited for an outburst of denunciation, for a criticism, at least, upon the delinquent officers; but I waited in vain: so far from a word of censure escaping his lips, he soon added, that his first remark might not appear uncharitable, 'I do not know that I could have given different orders had I been with them myself: I have not fully made up my mind how I should behave when Minie-balls were whistling, and those great oblong shells shrieking, in my ear. I might run away.'" *

He spoke and acted with the wisdom of the serpent and the harmlessness of the dove whenever practicable. In August, 1862, he said, when, as one of the peculiar trials incident to his position, he stood, as it were, between contending parties, "Gen. McClellan's attitude is such, that, in the very selfishness of his nature, he cannot but wish to be successful, and I hope he will; and the Secretary of War is in precisely the same situa-

* Col. Deming's Address.

tion. . . . Gen. McClellan has sometimes asked for things which the Secretary of War did not give him. Gen. McClellan is not to blame for asking what he wanted and needed; and the Secretary of War is not to blame for not giving when he had none to give." Thus he sought to conciliate opposers and fault-finders; but still he must have suffered from the unrest such cavilling induces. He had a similar trial when he removed Gen. Curtis; and so in March, 1863, he wrote, "Your despatch is received. It is very painful to me that you, in Missouri, cannot or will not settle your factional quarrel among yourselves. I have been tormented with it beyond endurance, for months, by both sides. Neither side pays the least respect to my appeals to your reason: I am now compelled to take hold of the case."

When he issued his immortal proclamation, there were fault-finders to whom he was compelled to reply: "If, now, the pressure of war should call off our forces from New Orleans to defend some other point, what is to prevent the masters from reducing the blacks to slavery again? for I am told, that whenever the rebels take any black prisoners, free or slave, they immediately auction them off (they did so with those they took from a boat in the Tennessee River a few days ago); and then I am very ungenerously attacked for it. For instance: When, after the late battles at and near Bull Run, an expedition went out from Washington, under a flag of truce, to bury the dead and bring in the wounded, and the rebels seized the blacks who went along to help, and sent them into slavery, Horace Greeley said in his paper that 'the Government would probably do nothing about it.' What *could* I do?"

It is plain that the President felt keenly the censures of those who misunderstood his motives, and did not agree with his plans.

The President suffered, too, when the fate of war overtook his personal friends, and they that drew the sword perished by the sword. With his great heart of sympathy, he felt for all who mourned the loss of father, son, brother, husband, or friend; but there must, of course, have been for him peculiar trials in the death of those whom he personally knew and loved. Col. Baker, the senator from California, who deemed it his duty to lay aside the toga, and buckle on the sword, was one of the friends whom he was called to lose when our brave boys were defeated at Ball's Bluff.* A lady correspondent of the "San-Francisco Bulletin" thus alludes to a conversation which she had with the President, at the Soldiers' Home, near Washington, in which they referred to Col. Baker, and felt his loss: —

"I had always noticed that the bare mention of our California cemetery filled the minds of those who heard it with a solemn sense of awe and sorrow, — Lone Mountain! It seemed to rise before them out of the quiet sea, a vast mausoleum from the hand of God wherein to lay the dead. I was not astonished, therefore, when Mr. Lincoln alluded to it in this way, and gave, in a few deep-toned words, a eulogy on one of its most honored dead, — Col. Baker. Having witnessed the impressive spectacle of that glorious soldier's funeral, I gave him the meagre outline one can convey in words, of something, which, having been once seen, must remain a living picture in the memory forever. I tried to picture the solemn hush that lay like a pall on the spirit of the people while the grand procession wound its mournful length through the streets of the city, out on that

* Once Lincoln said the keenest blow of all the war was at an early stage, when the disaster of Ball's Bluff and the death of his beloved Baker smote him like a whirlwind from the desert.

tear-stained road, to the gate of the cemetery, where the body passed beneath the prophetic words of the most eloquent soul, 'Hither, in the future ages, they shall bring,' &c.

"When I spoke of the California apostle, Starr King, I saw how strong a chord I had touched in the great appreciative heart I addressed; and, giving a weak dilution of that wondrous draught of soul-lit eloquence, — that funeral hymn uttered by the priest of God over the sacred ashes of the advocate and soldier of liberty, whose thrilling threnody seems yet to linger in the sighing wind that waves the grass upon the soil made sacred by the treasure it received that day, — I felt strangely impressed as to the power and grandeur of that mind whose thoughts at second-hand, and haltingly given from memory, should move and touch the soul of such a man as Abraham Lincoln, as I saw it touched when he listened. It is the electric chain with which all genius and grandeur of soul whatsoever is bound; the free-masonry by which spirit hails spirit, though unseen. Now they all three meet where it is not seeing 'through a glass darkly,' but in the light of a perfect day."

The President was also and earlier personally afflicted, when, —

"Down where the patriot-army,
Near Potomac's tide,
Guards the glorious cause of Freedom,
Gallant Ellsworth died."

This brave and remarkably efficient young officer had been associated with the President when in Illinois; and at his funeral, which took place at the White House, the President was the chief mourner.

"Bold leader of the Zouave band! —
A name not written in the sand, —
Thou, dying, leav'st thy native land.

In Freedom's annals, side by side,
Thy name with Warren's is allied, —
The tyrant's dread, the patriot's pride!

The marble shaft for each we raise;
For each the poet pours his lays;
Time wreathes for both unwithering bays." *

But there was one stroke nearer home than all which were among the peculiar trials of our beloved Chief Magistrate. Once before, the nation sympathized with a father and mother who must tread the halls of the White House without the echoes of familiar footsteps at their side. President Pierce and President Lincoln both knew what it was to wear the robe of royalty, as it were, over a bleeding heart. The nation sympathized when little Willie Lincoln died; and on the day when, all over the land, citizens assembled, in response to the President's request, that the "Farewell Address" of Washington might be read, the head of the nation sat bowed with grief over the dear remains of his darling son.

The following was addressed to the Senate and House; but Congress had adjourned before it was delivered:—

"The President of the United States was last evening plunged into affliction by the death of a beloved child. The heads of departments, in consideration of this distressing event, have thought it would be agreeable to Congress and to the American people that the official and private buildings occupied by them should not be illuminated on the evening of the 22d inst.

"WILLIAM H. SEWARD.
SALMON P. CHASE.
E. M. STANTON.
GIDEON WELLES.
EDWARD P. BATES.
M. BLAIR."

* Mary Webb.

And this official communication was but one among many tokens that the people felt deep sympathy with their beloved President in his paternal grief.

One of the leading newspapers thus refers to the last sad rites over the early-called: —

"The funeral of Master William Wallace Lincoln occurred yesterday at the White House, at two, P.M. His friends and acquaintances were previously allowed the sad pleasure of a last look in the Green Room, where lay his remains, clothed in accustomed pants and jacket, with white stockings and low shoes, with white collar and wristbands turned over the dark cloth of the jacket.

"On his breast rested a wreath of flowers; another lay near his feet; while a beautiful bouquet was held in his hand: the flowers composing the wreaths and bouquet being the queenly camellias; while azalias, and sprigs of mignonette, were disposed about the body.

"The beautiful bouquet in his hand was reserved for his sorrowing mother. A plain, metallic case of imitation rosewood was inscribed, 'William Wallace Lincoln, born Dec. 21, 1850; died Feb. 20, 1862.' The frames of the mirrors in the east and green rooms were covered with black crape; and the glass, with white crape. The funeral-service was performed by the pastor of the President, Rev. Dr. Gurley, in a very impressive manner.

"There were present members of the Cabinet, foreign ministers, members of Congress, army and navy officers, and many citizens and ladies. After the services, the body was placed in a vault at the Oak-Hill Cemetery, at Georgetown." *

Little did any then assembled think, as they looked upon the motionless form of the departed son, that, ere

* "National Republican."

many months, that precious dust would be removed and borne in a funeral procession, the like of which was never seen before; and that the father's form, now convulsed with grief, would then be lying cold and still in the sarcophagus where a nation had tearfully laid him, and move, side by side with the son, in an almost triumphal march, to a final resting-place in the Western land they loved, and from whence they came to the Nation's capitol and the Nation's heart.

At that far-off grave-side, the voice of the living preacher proclaimed the fact, which all men had learned by the rich experiences of four sad years, that the heart of the martyred President was tenderness itself; and it was pierced by the arrow of bereavement at the death of "Little Willie." Said the bishop then officiating,—

"In his domestic life, he was exceedingly kind and affectionate. He was a devoted husband and father. During his presidential term, he lost his second son Willie. To an officer of the army he said, not long since, 'Do you ever find yourself talking with the dead?' and added, 'Since Willie's death, I catch myself every day involuntarily talking with him, as if he were with me.'"

Even that trial was a blessing to his spirit. Heaven seemed nearer, doubtless, because Willie had passed through the gate. And, most assuredly, all the trials which our President was called to endure, though they were "not joyous, but grievous," yet they wrought in him "the peaceable fruits of righteousness," and day by day he was ripening for the immortality into which he was so soon to enter.

CHAPTER VIII.

REMARKABLE DOCUMENTS.

"Now 'Onward to Freedom!' let this be the cry;
For justice and truth are born never to die:
Go, say to the minions of slavery's thrall
That all men are brothers, and God over all!
Though stern be the struggle, the triumph we'll tell
In the jubilant peal of the Liberty-bell!"

MARY WEBB.

"Heaven and earth shall pass away; but my words shall not pass away." — THE LORD JESUS (Luke xxi. 33).

THERE are some documents that will never be forgotten, whose words will never lose their power. England's "Magna Charta" and America's "Declaration of Independence" are among them. So also is the "Emancipation Proclamation" of Abraham Lincoln. While this volume is not to be crowded with official documents, a chapter must, at least, be given to some papers written by the hand that held the sceptre and the sword in this nation during the stormy period of the Rebellion, and which are unmistakably stamped with his own nobleness of soul.

First in order of time comes President Lincoln's

FIRST INAUGURAL ADDRESS.

"FELLOW-CITIZENS OF THE UNITED STATES, — In compliance with a custom as old as the Government itself, I appear before you to address you briefly, and to take, in your presence, the oath prescribed by the Constitution of the United States to be taken by the President before he enters on the execution of his office.

"I do not consider it necessary, at present, for me to discuss those matters of administration about which there is no special anxiety or excitement. Apprehension seems to exist among the people of the Southern States, that, by the accession of a Republican Administration, their property, and their peace and personal security, are to be endangered. There has never been any reasonable cause for such apprehension. Indeed, the most ample evidence to the contrary has all the while existed, and been open to their inspection. It is found in nearly all the published speeches of him who now addresses you. I do but quote from one of those speeches when I declare that 'I have no purpose, directly or indirectly, to interfere with the institution of slavery in the States where it exists.' I believe I have no lawful right to do so; and I have no inclination to do so. Those who nominated and elected me did so with the full knowledge that I had made this and made many similar declarations, and had never recanted them; and, more than this, they placed in the platform, for my acceptance, and as a law to themselves and to me, the clear and emphatic resolution which I now read:—

"'*Resolved*, That the maintenance inviolate of the rights of the States, and especially the right of each State to order and control its own domestic institutions according to its own judgment exclusively, is essential to that balance of power on which the perfection and endurance of our political fabric depend; and we denounce the lawless invasion, by armed force, of the soil of any State or Territory, no matter under what pretext, as among the greatest of crimes.'

"I now reiterate these sentiments; and, in doing so, I only press upon the public attention the most conclusive evidence of which the case is susceptible,—that the property, peace, and security of no section are to be in any wise endangered by the now incoming Administration.

"I add, too, that all the protection which, consistently with the Constitution and the laws, can be given, will be cheerfully given to all the States when lawfully demanded, for whatever cause, as cheerfully to one section as to another.

"There is much controversy about the delivering-up of fugitives from service or labor. The clause I now read is as plainly written in the Constitution as any other of its provisions: —

"'No person held to service or labor in one State, under the laws thereof, escaping into another, shall, in consequence of any law or regulation therein, be discharged from such service or labor, but shall be delivered up on claim of the party to whom such service or labor may be due.'

"'It is scarcely questioned that this provision was intended by those who made it for the reclaiming of what we call fugitive slaves; and the intention of the lawgiver is the law.

"All members of Congress swear their support to the whole Constitution, — to this provision as well as any other. To the proposition, then, that slaves whose cases come within the terms of this clause 'shall be delivered up,' their oaths are unanimous. Now, if they would make the effort in good temper, could they not, with nearly equal unanimity, frame and pass a law by means of which to keep good that unanimous oath?

"There is some difference of opinion whether this clause should be enforced by National or by State authority; but surely that difference is not a very material one. If the slave is to be surrendered, it can be of but little consequence to him or to others by which authority it is done; and should any one, in any case, be content that this oath shall go unkept, on a merely unsubstantial controversy as to how it shall be kept?

"Again: in any law upon this subject, ought not all the safeguards of liberty known in civilized and humane jurisprudence to be so that a free man be not, in any case, surrendered as a slave? And might it not be well at the same time to provide by law for the enforcement of that clause in the Constitution which guarantees that 'the citizens of each State shall be entitled to all the privileges and immunities of citizens in the several States'?

"I take the official oath to-day with no mental reservations, and with no purpose to construe the Constitution or laws by any hypercritical rules. While I do not choose now to specify particular acts of Congress as proper to be enforced, I do suggest that it will be much safer for all, both in official and private stations, to conform to, and abide by, all those acts which stand unrepealed, than to violate any of them, trusting to find impunity in having them held to be unconstitutional.

"It is seventy-two years since the first inauguration of a President under our National Constitution. During that period, fifteen different and very distinguished citizens have, in succession, administered the executive branch of the Government. They have conducted it through many perils, and, generally, with great success. Yet, with all this scope for precedent, I now enter upon the same task for the brief constitutional term of four years under great and peculiar difficulties. A disruption of the Federal Union, heretofore only menaced, is now formidably attempted. I hold that in the contemplation of universal law, and of the Constitution, the Union of these States is perpetual. Perpetuity is implied, if not expressed, in the fundamental law of all national governments. It is safe to assert that no government proper ever had a provision in its organic law for its own termination. Continue to execute all the express provisions of our National Constitution, and the Union will endure forever; it being impossible to destroy it, except by some action not provided for in the instrument itself. Again: if the United States be not a government proper, but an association of States in the nature of a contract merely, can it, as a contract, be peaceably unmade by less than all the parties who made it? One party to a contract may violate it,—break it, so to speak; but does it not require all to lawfully rescind it? Descending from these general principles, we find the proposition, that, in legal contemplation, the Union is perpetual, confirmed by the history of the Union itself. The Union is much older than the Constitution. It was formed, in fact, by the Articles of Association in 1774. It was matured and continued in the Declaration of Independence in 1776. It was further matured, and the faith of all the then thirteen States expressly plighted and engaged that it should be perpetual, by the Articles of the Confederation in 1778; and finally, in 1787, one of the declared objects for establishing the Constitution was to form a more perfect Union. But, if the destruction of the Union by one or by a part only of the States be lawfully possible, the Union is less than before, the Constitution having lost the vital element of perpetuity. It follows from these views that no State upon its own mere motion can lawfully get out of the Union; that resolves and ordinances to that effect are legally void; and that acts of violence within any State or States against the United States are insurrectionary or revolutionary, according to circumstances. I therefore consider, that, in view of the Constitution and the laws, the Union is unbroken; and, to the extent of my ability, I shall take care, as the Constitution itself expressly enjoins upon me, that the laws of the Union shall be faithfully executed in all the States. Doing this, which I deem to be only a simple duty on my part, I shall perfectly perform it, so far as is practicable, unless my rightful masters, the American people, shall withhold the requisition, or, in some authoritative measure, direct the contrary. I trust this will not be regarded as a menace, but only as the declared purpose of the Union, that it will constitutionally defend and maintain itself. In doing this, there need be no bloodshed or violence; and there shall be none, unless it is forced upon the national authority. The power confided to me *will be used to hold, occupy, and possess the property and places* belonging to the Government, and collect the duties and imposts; but, beyond what may be necessary for those objects, there will be no invasion, no using of force against or among the people anywhere. Where hostility to the United States shall be so great and so universal as to prevent competent Federal citizens from holding office, there will be no attempt to force obnoxious strangers upon the people who object. While the strict legal right may exist of the Government to enforce the exercise of these offices, the attempt to do so would be so irritating and so nearly impracticable withal, that I deem it best to forego, for the time, the uses of such offices. The mails, unless repelled, will continue to be furnished in all parts of the Union. So far as possible, the people everywhere shall have that sense of perfect security which is most favorable to calm thought and reflection.

"The course here indicated will be followed, unless current events and experience shall show a modification or change to be proper; and, in every case and exigency, my best discretion will be exercised according to the circumstances actually existing, and with a view and hope of a peaceful solution of the national troubles, and the restoration of fraternal sympathies and affections.

"That there are persons in one section or another who seek to destroy the Union at all events, and are glad of any pretext to do it, I will neither affirm nor deny. But, if there be such, I need address no word to them. To those, however, who really love the Union, may I not speak before entering upon so grave a matter as the destruction of our national fabric, with all its benefits, its memories, and its hopes? Would it not be well to ascertain why we do it? Will you hazard so desperate a step, while any portion of the ills you fly from have no real existence? Will you, while the certain ills you fly to are greater than all the real ones you fly from, — will you risk the commission of so fearful a mistake? All profess to be content in the Union if all constitutional rights can be maintained. Is it true, then, that any right plainly written in the Constitution has been denied? I think not. Happily the human mind is so constituted, that no party can reach to the audacity of doing this.

"Think, if you can, of a single instance in which a plainly written provision of the Constitution has ever been denied. If, by mere force of numbers, a majority should deprive a minority of any clearly written constitutional right, it might, in a moral point of view, justify revolution: it certainly would if such right were a vital one. But such is not our case.

"All the vital rights of minorities and of individuals are so plainly assured to them by affirmations and negations, guaranties and prohibitions, in the Constitution, that controversies never arise concerning them. But no organic law can ever be framed with a provision specifically applicable to every question which may occur in practical administration. No foresight can anticipate, nor any document of reasonable length contain, express provisions for all possible questions. Shall fugitives from labor be surrendered by National, or by State authorities? The Constitution does not expressly say. Must Congress protect slavery in the Territories? The Constitution does not expressly say. From questions of this nature spring all our constitutional controversies, and we divide upon them into majorities and minorities.

"If the minority will not acquiesce, the majority must, or the Government must cease. There is no alternative for continuing the Government but acquiescence on the one side or the other. If a minority in such a case will secede rather than acquiesce, they make a precedent, which, in turn, will ruin and divide them; for a minority of their own will secede from them whenever a majority refuses to be controlled by such a minority. For instance, why not any portion of a new confederacy a year or two hence arbitrarily secede again, precisely as portions of the present Union now claim to secede from it? All who cherish disunion sentiments are now being educated to the exact temper of doing this. Is there such perfect identity of interests among the States to compose a new Union as to produce harmony only, and prevent renewed secession? Plainly the central idea of secession is the essence of anarchy.

"A majority held in restraint by constitutional check and limitation, and always changing easily with deliberate changes of popular opinions and sentiments, is the only true sovereign of a free people. Whoever rejects it, does, of necessity, fly to anarchy or to despotism. Unanimity is impossible: the rule of a majority, as a permanent arrangement, is wholly inadmissible; so that, rejecting the majority principle, anarchy or despotism, in some form, is all that is left.

"I do not forget the position assumed by some, that constitutional questions are to be decided by the Supreme Court; nor do I deny that such decisions must be binding in any case upon the parties to a suit, as to the object of that suit; while they are also entitled to a very high respect and consideration in all parallel cases by all other departments of the Government: and while it is obviously possible that such decision may be erroneous in any given case, still the evil effect following it being limited to that particular case, with the chance that it may be overruled, and never become a precedent for other cases, can better be borne than could the evils of a different practice.

"At the same time, the candid citizen must confess, that, if the policy of the Government upon the vital question affecting the whole people is to be irrevocably fixed by the decisions of the Supreme Court, the instant they are made, as in ordinary litigation between parties in personal actions, the people will have ceased to be their own masters, unless having to that extent practically resigned their government into the hands of that eminent tribunal.

"Nor is there in this view any assault upon the court or the judges. It is a duty from which they may not shrink, to decide cases properly brought before them; and it is no fault of theirs if others seek to turn their decisions to political purposes. One section of our country believes slavery is right, and ought to be extended, while the other believes it is wrong, and ought not to be extended; and this is the only substantial dispute; and the fugitive-slave clause of the Constitution, and the law for the suppression of the foreign slave-trade, are each as well enforced, perhaps, as any law can ever be in a community where the moral sense of the people imperfectly supports the law itself. The great body of the people abide by the dry legal obligation in both cases, and a few break over in each. This, I think, cannot be perfectly cured; and it would be worse in both cases after the separation of the sections than before. The foreign slave-trade, now imperfectly suppressed, would be ultimately revived, without restriction, in one section; while fugitive slaves, now only partially surrendered, would not be surrendered at all by the other.

"Physically speaking, we cannot separate; we cannot remove our respective sections from each other, nor build an impassable wall between them. A husband and wife may be divorced, and go out of the presence and beyond the reach of each other; but the different parts of our country cannot do this. They cannot but remain face to face; and intercourse, either amicable or hostile, must continue between them. Is it possible, then, to make that intercourse more advantageous or more satisfactory after separation than before? Can aliens make treaties easier than friends can make laws? Can treaties be more faithfully enforced between aliens than laws can among friends? Suppose you go to war, you cannot fight always; and when, after much loss on both sides, and no gain on either, you cease fighting, the identical questions as to terms of intercourse are again upon you.

"This country, with its institutions, belongs to the people who inhabit it. Whenever they shall grow weary of the existing government, they can exercise their constitutional right of amending, or their revolutionary right to dismember or overthrow it. I cannot be ignorant of the fact, that many worthy and patriotic citizens are desirous of having the National Constitution amended. While I make no recommendation of amendment, I fully recognize the full authority of the people over the whole subject, to be exercised in either of the modes prescribed in the instrument itself; and I should, under existing circumstances, favor, rather than oppose, a fair opportunity being afforded the people to act upon it.

"I will venture to add, that, to me, the convention mode seems preferable, in that it allows amendments to originate with the people themselves, instead of only permitting them to take or reject propositions originated by others not especially chosen for the purpose, and which might not be precisely such as they would wish either to accept or refuse. I understand that a proposed amendment to the Constitution (which amendment, however, I have not seen) has passed Congress, to the effect that the Federal Government shall never interfere with the domestic institutions of States, including that of persons held to service. To avoid misconstruction of what I have said, I depart from my purpose, not to speak of particular amendments, so far as to say, that, holding such a provision now to be implied constitutional law, I have no objection to its being made express and irrevocable.

"The Chief Magistrate derives all his authority from the people, and they have conferred none upon him to fix the terms for the separation of the States. The people themselves can do this if they choose; but the Executive, as such, has nothing to do with it. His duty is to administer the present Government as it came to his hands, and to transmit it, unimpaired by him, to his successor. Why should there not be a patient confidence in the ultimate justice of the people? Is there any better or equal hope in the world? In our present differences, is either party without faith of being in the right? If the Almighty Ruler of nations, with his eternal truth and justice, be on your side of the North, or on yours of the South, that truth and that justice will surely prevail by the judgment of this great tribunal,—the American people.

"By the frame of the Government under which we live, this same people have wisely given their public servants but little power for mischief, and have, with equal wisdom, provided for the return of that little to their own hands at very short intervals. While the people retain their virtue and vigilance, no administration, by any extreme wickedness or folly, can very seriously injure the Government in the short space of four years.

"My countrymen, one and all, think calmly and well upon this whole subject. Nothing valuable can be lost by taking time.

"If there be an object to hurry any of you, in hot haste, to a step which you would never take deliberately, that object will be frustrated by taking time; but no good object can be frustrated by it.

"Such of you as are now dissatisfied still have the old Constitution unimpaired, and on the sensitive point, the laws of your own framing under it; while the new administration will have no immediate power, if it would, to change either.

"If it were admitted that you who are dissatisfied hold the right side in the dispute, there is still no single reason for precipitate action. Intelligence, patriotism, Christianity, and a firm reliance on Him who has never yet forsaken this favored land, are still competent to adjust in the best way all our present difficulties.

"In your hands, my dissatisfied fellow-countrymen, and not in mine, is the momentous issue of civil war. The Government will not assail you.

"You can have no conflict without being yourselves the aggressors. You have no oath registered in heaven to destroy the Government, while I shall have the most solemn one to 'preserve, protect, and defend it.'

"I am loath to close. We are not enemies, but friends. We must not be enemies. Though passion may have strained, it must not break, our bonds of affection.

"The mystic cords of memory, stretching from every battle-field and patriot grave to every living heart and hearthstone all over this broad land, will yet swell the chorus of the Union when again touched, as surely they will be, by the better angels of our nature."

Inaugural addresses had been written by all his predecessors; but, in scarcely a month from the time when he delivered that address, the President had occasion to write a paper differing from any they had ever written. It was a call for troops, and summoned Congress to assemble; for *civil war* had begun. How many tears greeted that paper, as hearts that shrank from scenes of carnage pictured to themselves, as they read it, the horrors of a war which seemed inevitable!

PROCLAMATION.

Whereas the laws of the United States have been for some time past, and now are, opposed, and the execution thereof obstructed, in the States of South Carolina, Georgia, Alabama, Florida, Mississippi, Louisiana, and Texas, by combinations too powerful to be suppressed by the ordinary course of judicial proceedings, or by the power vested in the marshals by law: now therefore, I,

Abraham Lincoln, President of the United States, in virtue of the power in me vested by the Constitution and the laws, have thought fit to call forth, and hereby do call forth, the militia of the several States of the Union, to the aggregate number of 75,000, in order to suppress said combinations, and to cause the laws to be duly executed.

The details for this object will be immediately communicated to the State authorities through the War Department. I appeal to all loyal citizens to favor, facilitate, and aid this effort to maintain the honor, the integrity, and existence of our National Union, and the perpetuity of popular government, and to redress wrongs already long enough endured. I deem it proper to say that the first service assigned to the forces hereby called forth will probably be to repossess the forts, places, and property which have been seized from the Union; and in every event the utmost care will be observed, consistently with the objects aforesaid, to avoid any devastation, any destruction of or interference with property, or any disturbance of peaceful citizens of any part of the country; and I hereby command the persons composing the combinations aforesaid to disperse and retire peaceably to their respective abodes within twenty days from this date.

Deeming that the present condition of public affairs presents an extraordinary occasion, I do hereby, in virtue of the power in me vested by the Constitution, convene both Houses of Congress. The senators and representatives are, therefore, summoned to assemble at their respective chambers at twelve o'clock noon, on Thursday, the fourth day of July next, then and there to consider and determine such measures as, in their wisdom, the public safety and interest seem to demand.

In witness whereof, I have hereunto set my hand, and caused the seal of the United States to be affixed.

Done at the city of Washington, this fifteenth day of April, in the year of our Lord one thousand eight hundred and sixty-one, and of the independence of the United States the eighty-fifth.

ABRAHAM LINCOLN.

By the President:

WILLIAM H. SEWARD, *Secretary of State.*

This proclamation was followed by one ordering the blockade of the Southern ports, and issued on the day when the first blood was shed for Liberty and Union.

Subsequently, the President sent the following letter (interesting particularly as showing his modesty and peace-loving spirit) to the Governor of Maryland and the Mayor of Baltimore: —

WASHINGTON, April 20, 1861.

GOVERNOR HICKS AND MAYOR BROWN. *Gentlemen,* — Your letter by Messrs. Bond, Dobbin, and Brome, is received. I tender you both my sincere thanks for your efforts to keep the peace in the trying situation in which you are placed. For the future, troops *must* be brought here; but I make no point of bringing them *through* Baltimore.

Without any military knowledge myself, of course I must leave details to Gen. Scott. He hastily said this morning, in presence of those gentlemen, 'March them *around* Baltimore, and not through it.'

I sincerely hope the general, on fuller reflection, will consider this practical and proper, and that you will not object to it. By this a collision of the people of Baltimore with the troops will be avoided, unless they go out of the way to seek it. I hope you will exert your influence to prevent this. Now and ever, I shall do all in my power for peace, consistently with the maintenance of government. Your obedient servant,

A. LINCOLN.

In July, the President sent his first message to Congress,—an interesting document, but too long to be inserted here. In it he remarked forcibly, "The Union must be preserved, and hence all indispensable means must be employed." It may be, that, even then, he was looking forward to a day when he might pronounce slavery at an end in the United States; for "there yet remains in the minds of men who were acquainted with Mr. Lincoln in the spring and summer of 1861 the recollection of expressions made by him, which indicate that there were then vague thoughts in his mind that it might be his lot under Providence to bring the slaves of the country out of their bondage."*

On the 12th of August, the President issued a proclamation, eminently appropriate in expression, and Christian in tone, for a day of fasting and prayer, as follows:—

"*Whereas* a joint committee of both Houses of Congress has waited on the President of the United States, and requested him to 'recommend a day of public humiliation, prayer, and fasting, to be observed by the people of the United States with religious solemnities, and the offering of fervent supplications to Almighty God for the safety and welfare of these States, his blessing on their arms, and a speedy restoration of peace;'—

"*And whereas* it is fit and becoming in all people, at

* Ex-Governor Boutwell's Eulogy.

all times, to acknowledge and revere the supreme government of God; to bow in humble submission to his chastisements; to confess and deplore their sins and transgressions, in the full conviction that the fear of the Lord is the beginning of wisdom, and to pray, with all fervency and contrition, for the pardon of their past offences, and for a blessing upon their present and prospective action; —

"*And whereas*, when our own beloved country, once, by the blessing of God, united, prosperous, and happy, is now afflicted with faction and civil war, it is peculiarly fit for us to recognize the hand of God in this terrible visitation, and in sorrowful remembrance of our own faults and crimes as a nation, and as individuals, to humble ourselves before him, and to pray for his mercy; to pray that we may be spared further punishment, though most justly deserved; that our arms may be blessed, and made effectual for the re-establishment of law, order, and peace throughout the wide extent of our country; and that the inestimable boon of civil and religious liberty, earned under his guidance and blessing by the labors and sufferings of our fathers, may be restored in all its original excellence: —

"*Therefore* I, Abraham Lincoln, President of the United States, do appoint the last Thursday in September next as a day of humiliation, prayer, and fasting for all the people of the nation. And I do earnestly recommend to all the people, and especially to all ministers and teachers of religion of all denominations, and to all heads of families, to observe and keep that day according to their several creeds and modes of worship, in all humility, and with all religious solemnity, to the end that the united prayer of the nation may ascend to the throne of Grace, and bring down plentiful blessings upon our country.

"In testimony whereof, I have hereunto set my hand, and caused the seal of the United States to be [L. S.] affixed, this twelfth day of August, A.D. 1861, and of the independence of the United States of America the eighty-sixth.

"ABRAHAM LINCOLN.

"By the President:

"WILLIAM H. SEWARD, *Secretary of State.*"

The day was duly kept, and fervent prayers ascended, asking safety for the nation, and wisdom for its head.

In the latter part of the same month, Gen. Frémont declared martial law in Missouri, and ordered the property of secessionists to be confiscated, and their slaves to be declared free men; but the President deemed it his duty to so modify the order to liberate and confiscate, as not to have Gen. Frémont transcend the provisions on that theme contained in a Congressional act just passed. Mr. Lincoln has been much censured for this; but he acted according to his best judgment. He did not think the times were ripe for such a noble act of mercy and justice.

In December he sent another message to Congress, which was an eminently conservative document, and gave satisfaction to all loyal hearts.

In March following he sent another message, recommending gradual emancipation; and on the 16th of April, 1862, he consummated an act which had for many years been one of his most favorite projects by sending into Congress the following message, announcing that his signature was affixed to the document which abolished slavery in the District of Columbia:—

"FELLOW-CITIZENS OF THE SENATE AND HOUSE OF REPRESENTATIVES,—The act entitled 'An act for the release of certain persons held to service or labor in the District of Columbia' has this day been approved and signed.

"I have never doubted the constitutional authority of Congress to abolish slavery in this District, and I have ever desired to see the national capital freed from the institution in some satisfactory way. Hence there has never been in my mind any question upon the subject, except the one of expediency, arising in view of all the circumstances. If there be matters within and about this act which might have taken a course or shape more satisfactory to my judgment, I do not attempt to specify them. I am gratified that the two principles of compensation and colonization are both recognized and practically applied in the act.

"In the matter of compensation, it is provided that claims may be presented within ninety days from the passage of the act, but not thereafter; and there is no saving for minors, *femmes coverts*, insane, or absent persons. I presume this is an omission by mere oversight; and I recommend that it be supplied by an amendatory or supplemental act. "ABRAHAM LINCOLN."

The friends of freedom everywhere rejoiced when this good deed was done; and Whittier, the "poet of the slave," poured out his soul in rhythmic words of exultant joy. Still, though the President looked toward a day of freedom, in his opinion the hour had not struck in the belfry of the ages; and, therefore, when Gen. Hunter, like Gen. Frémont, transcended his powers in issuing an emancipation order, the President repudiated it in the following document:—

"*Whereas* there appears in the public prints what purports to be a proclamation of Major-Gen. Hunter, in the words and figures following; to wit,—

"HEADQUARTERS, DEPARTMENT OF THE SOUTH,
HILTON HEAD, S.C., May 9, 1862.

"GENERAL ORDERS, No. 11.

"The three States of Georgia, Florida, and South Carolina, comprising the Military Department of the South, having deliberately declared themselves no longer under the protection of the United States of America, and having taken up arms against the said United States, it becomes a military necessity to declare them under martial law. This was accordingly done on the twenty-fifth day of April, 1862. Slavery and martial law in a free country are altogether incompatible. The persons in these three States, Georgia, Florida, and South Carolina, heretofore held as slaves, are therefore declared forever free.

"DAVID HUNTER, *Major-Gen. Commanding.*

"Official:

"ED. W. SMITH, *Acting Asist. Adj.-Gen.*

"*And whereas* the same is producing some excitement and misunderstanding: —

"*Therefore* I, Abraham Lincoln, President of the United States, proclaim and declare that the Government of the United States had no knowledge or belief of an intention on the part of Gen. Hunter to issue such a proclamation, nor has it yet any authentic information that the document is genuine; and further, that neither Gen. Hunter, nor any other commander or person, has been authorized by the Government of the United States to make proclamation declaring the slaves of any State free; and that the supposed proclamation now in question, whether genuine or false, is altogether void, so far as respects such declaration.

"I further make known, that whether it be competent

for me, as Commander-in-chief of the Army and Navy, to declare the slaves of any State or States free, and whether at any time, or in any case, it shall have become a necessity indispensable to the maintenance of the Government to exercise such supposed power, are questions which, under my responsibility, I reserve to myself, and which I cannot feel justified in leaving to the decision of commanders in the field. These are totally different questions from those of police regulations in armies and camps.

"On the sixth day of March last, by a special message, I recommended to Congress the adoption of a joint resolution, to be substantially as follows: —

"'*Resolved,* That the United States ought to cooperate with any State which may adopt a gradual abolishment of slavery, giving to such State in its discretion to compensate for the inconveniences, public and private, produced by such change of system.'

"The resolution, in the language above quoted, was adopted by large majorities in both branches of Congress, and now stands an authentic, definite, and solemn proposal of the nation to the States and people most immediately interested in the subject-matter. To the people of these States I now earnestly appeal. I do not argue: I beseech you to make the arguments for yourselves. You cannot, if you would, be blind to the signs of the times. I beg of you a calm and enlarged consideration of them, ranging, if it may be, far above personal and partisan politics. This proposal makes common cause for a common object, casting no reproaches upon any. It acts not the Pharisee. The change it contemplates would come gently as the dews of heaven, not rending or wrecking any thing. Will you not embrace it? So much good has not been done by one effort in all past time, as, in the providence of God, it is now your high privilege to do. May the vast future not have to lament that you have neglected it!

"In witness whereof, I have hereunto set my hand, and caused the seal of the United States to be affixed.

"Done at the city of Washington, this nineteenth day of May, in the year of our Lord one thousand eight hundred and sixty-two, and of the independence of the United States the eighty-sixth.

"ABRAHAM LINCOLN.

"By the President:

"WILLIAM H. SEWARD, *Secretary of State.*"

On the 22d of September, Mr. Lincoln issued one of the two most important proclamations ever issued in our country. It announced to the slaves, who had been looking for the great jubilee, and felt that

"'Twas long, long, long on the way,"

that, on the coming New-Year's Day, he should pronounce them free. What human pen or voice can express the joy with which the announcement was hailed by the enslaved of our land? It was as follows: —

"I Abraham Lincoln, President of the United States of America, and Commander-in-chief of the Army and Navy thereof, do hereby proclaim and declare that hereafter, as heretofore, the war will be prosecuted for the object of practically restoring the constitutional relation between the United States and the people thereof in those States in which that relation is or may be suspended or disturbed; that it is my purpose, upon the next meeting of Congress, to again recommend the adoption of a practical measure tendering pecuniary aid to the free acceptance or rejection of all the slave States, so called, the people whereof may not then be in rebellion against the United States, and which States may then have voluntarily adopted, or thereafter may voluntarily adopt, the immediate or gradual abolishment of slavery within their respective limits; and that the effort to colonize persons of African descent, with their consent, upon the continent or elsewhere, with the previously obtained consent of the government existing there, will be continued; that on the first day of January, in the year of our Lord one thousand eight hundred and sixty-three, all persons held as slaves within any State, or any designated part of a State, the people whereof shall then be in rebellion against the United States, shall be then, thenceforward, and forever, free; and the Executive Government of the United States, including the military and naval authority thereof, will recognize and maintain the freedom of such persons, and will do no act or acts to repress such persons, or any of them, in any efforts they may make for their actual freedom; that the Executive will, on the first day of January aforesaid, by proclamation, designate the States, and parts of States, if any, in which the people thereof respectively shall then be in rebellion against the United States; and the fact that any State, or the people thereof, shall on that day be in good faith represented in the Congress of the United States by members chosen thereto, at elections wherein a majority of the qualified voters of such State shall have participated, shall, in the absence of strong countervailing testimony, be deemed conclusive evidence that such State and the people thereof have not been in rebellion against the United States.

"That attention is hereby called to an act of Congress, entitled 'An act to make an additional article of war,' approved March 13, 1862, and which act is in the words and figures following: —

"'*Be it enacted by the Senate and House of Representatives of the United States of America in Congress assembled,* That hereafter the following shall be promulgated as an additional article of war for the government of the army of the United States, and shall be observed and obeyed as such: —

"'*Article* —. All officers or persons of the military or naval service of the United States are prohibited from employing any of the forces under their respective commands for the purpose of returning fugitives from service or labor who may have escaped from any persons to whom such service or labor is claimed to be due; and any officer who shall be found guilty by a court-martial of violating this article shall be dismissed from the service.

"'*Sect.* 2. And be it further enacted, That this act shall take effect from and after its passage.'

"Also to the ninth and tenth sections of an act, entitled 'An act to suppress insurrection, to punish treason and rebellion, to seize and confiscate property of rebels, and for other purposes,' approved July 17, 1862; and which sections are in the words and figures following: —

"'*Sect.* 9. And be it further enacted, That all slaves of persons who shall hereafter be engaged in rebellion against the Government of the United States, or who shall in any way give aid or comfort thereto, escaping from such persons and taking refuge within the lines of the army, and all slaves captured from such persons or deserted by them, and coming under the control of the Government of the United States, and all slaves of such persons found on (or being within) any place occupied by rebel forces and afterwards occupied by the forces of of the United States, shall be deemed captives of war, and shall be forever free of their servitude, and not again held as slaves.

"'*Sect.* 10. And be it further enacted, That no slave escaping into any State, Territory, or the District of Columbia, from any of the States, shall be delivered up, or in any way impeded or hindered of his liberty, except for crime, or some offence against the laws, unless the person claiming said fugitive shall first make oath that the person to whom the labor or service of such fugitive is alleged to be due is his lawful owner, and has not been in arms against the United States in the present Rebellion, nor in any way given aid and comfort thereto; and no person engaged in the military or naval service of the United States shall, under any pretence whatever, assume to decide on the validity of the claim of any person to the service or labor of any other person, or surrender up any such person to the claimant, on pain of being dismissed from the service.'

"And I do hereby enjoin upon and order all persons engaged in the military and naval service of the United States to observe, obey, and enforce, within their respective spheres of service, the act and sections above recited.

"And the Executive will in due time recommend that all citizens of the United States, who shall have remained loyal thereto throughout the Rebellion, shall (upon the restoration of the constitutional relation between the United States and their respective States and people, if the relation shall have been suspended or disturbed) be compensated for all losses by acts of the United States, including the loss of slaves.

"In witness whereof, I have hereunto set my hand, and caused the seal of the United States to be affixed.

"Done at the city of Washington, this twenty-second day of September, in the year of our Lord one thousand eight hundred and sixty-two, and of the independence of the United States the eighty-seventh.

"ABRAHAM LINCOLN.

"By the President:

"WM. H. SEWARD, *Secretary of State.*"

Then came, in due season, *the* proclamation, which crowned its author with immortal fame, and made millions rejoice on earth and in heaven. Then sang Whittier, and all true hearts echoed: —

"Ring and swing,
Bells of joy! on morning's wing
Send the song of praise abroad;
With a sound of broken chains
Tell the nation that He reigns
Who alone is Lord and God!"

The following is

THE PROCLAMATION.

"*Whereas* on the twenty-second day of September, in the year of our Lord one thousand eight hundred and sixty-two, a proclamation was issued by the President of the United States, containing, among other things, the following; to wit, —

"'That on the first day of January, in the year of our Lord one thousand eight hundred and sixty-three, all persons held as slaves within any State, or designated part of a State, the people whereof shall then be in rebellion against the United States, shall be, then, thenceforth, and forever, free; and the Executive Government of the United States, including the military and naval authorities thereof, will recognize and maintain the freedom of such persons, and will do no act or acts to repress such persons, or any of them, in any efforts they may make for their actual freedom; —

"'That the Executive will, on the first day of January aforesaid, by proclamation, designate the States and parts of States, if any, in which the people therein respectively shall then be in rebellion against the United States; and the fact that any State, or the people thereof, shall on that day be in good faith represented in the Congress of the United States by members chosen thereto at elections wherein a majority of the qualified voters of such States shall have participated, shall, in the absence of strong countervailing testimony, be deemed conclusive evidence that such State, and the people thereof, are not then in rebellion against the United States:'—

"Now, therefore, I, Abraham Lincoln, President of the United States, by virtue of the power in me vested as Commander-in-chief of the Army and Navy of the United States in time of actual armed rebellion against the authority and government of the United States, and as a fit and necessary war measure for suppressing said rebellion, do, on this first day of January, in the year of our Lord one thousand eight hundred and sixty-three, and in accordance with my purpose so to do, publicly proclaimed for the full period of one hundred days from the day of the first above-mentioned order, designate as the States, and parts of States, wherein the people thereof respectively are this day in rebellion against the United States, the following; to wit, Arkansas, Texas, Louisiana, — except the parishes of St. Bernard, Plaquemines, Jefferson, St. John, St. Charles, St. James, Ascension, Assumption, Terre Bonne, Lafourche, St. Mary, St. Martin, and Orleans, including the city of New Orleans, — Mississippi, Alabama, Florida, Georgia, South Carolina, North Carolina, and Virginia, except the forty-eight counties designated as West Virginia, and also the counties of Berkeley, Accomac, Northampton, Elizabeth City, York, Princess Ann, and Norfolk, including the cities of Norfolk and Portsmouth, and which excepted parts are, for the present, left precisely as if this proclamation were not issued.

"And by virtue of the power, and for the purpose aforesaid, I do order and declare that all persons held as slaves within said designated States, and parts of States, are, and henceforward shall be, free; and that the Executive Government of the United States, including the military and naval authorities thereof, will recognize and maintain the freedom of said persons.

"And I hereby enjoin upon the people so declared to be free to abstain from all violence, unless in necessary self-defence; and I recommend to them, that in all cases, when allowed, they labor faithfully for reasonable wages.

"And I further declare and make known that such persons of suitable condition will be received into the armed service of the United States to garrison forts, positions, stations, and other places, and to man vessels of all sorts in said service.

"And upon this, sincerely believed to be an act of justice, warranted by the Constitution, upon military necessity, I invoke the considerate judgment of mankind and the gracious favor of Almighty God.

"In witness whereof, I have hereunto set my hand, and caused the seal of the United States to be affixed.

[L. S.] "Done at the city of Washington, this first day of January, in the year of our Lord one thousand eight hundred and sixty-three, and of the independence of the United States of America the eighty-seventh.

"ABRAHAM LINCOLN.

"By the President:

"WILLIAM H. SEWARD, *Secretary of State.*"

What is the estimate placed upon this proclamation? Hear the words of him who was about to commit the remains of its author to the tomb: —

"The great act of the mighty chieftain, on which his fame shall rest long after his frame shall moulder away, is that of giving freedom to a race. We have all been taught to revere the sacred characters. Among them Moses stand pre-eminently high. He received the law from God, and his name is honored among the hosts of heaven. Was not his greatest act the delivering of three millions of his kindred out of bondage? Yet we may assert that Abraham Lincoln, by his proclamation, liberated more enslaved people than ever Moses set free, and those not of his kindred or his race. Such a power or such an opportunity God has seldom given to man. When other events shall have been forgotten; when this world shall have become a network of republics; when every throne shall be swept from the face of the earth; when literature shall enlighten all minds; when the claims of humanity shall be recognized everywhere; this act shall still be conspicuous in the ages of history. We are thankful that God gave to Abraham Lincoln the decision and wisdom and grace to issue that proclamation, which stands high above all other papers which have been penned by uninspired men." *

President Lincoln, as elsewhere shown, had always advocated freedom for all. He distinctly declared his views in regard to slavery as an evil which he would have been glad to see removed, even if it had not been a military necessity to pronounce the slaves of the enemy free. He says himself, "I am naturally antislavery. If slavery is not wrong, nothing is wrong. I cannot

* Bishop Simpson.

remember when I did not see, think, and feel that it was wrong; and yet I have never understood that the presidency conferred upon me an unrestricted right to act officially upon this judgment and feeling. It was in the oath I took, that I would, to the best of my ability, preserve, protect, and defend the Constitution of the United States. I could not take the office without taking the oath; nor was it in my view that I might take an oath to get power, and break the oath in using the power. I understood too, that, in ordinary civil administration, this oath even forbade me to practically indulge my primary abstract judgment on the moral question of slavery. I had publicly declared this many times, and in many ways; and I aver, that, to this day, I have done no official act in mere deference to my abstract judgment and feeling on slavery. I did understand, however, that my oath to preserve the Constitution to the best of my ability imposed upon me the duty of preserving, by every indispensable means, that Government, that nation, of which that Constitution was the organic law."

We see here the President's cautious adherence to the path of duty. He would not allow even his convictions of right under other circumstances to interfere with the strict discharge of his duties as President. When some who loved freedom, and pitied the slave, urged upon him a more rapid stride toward emancipation, he answered them in the spirit of the following letter, written by him to Hon. Horace Greeley, Aug. 22, 1862:—

"DEAR SIR,—I have just read yours of the 19th inst., addressed to myself through the 'New-York Tribune.'

"If there be in it any statements or assumptions of fact which I may know to be erroneous, I do not now and here controvert them.

"If there be any inferences which I may believe to be falsely drawn, I do not now and here argue against them.

"If there be perceptible in it an impatient and dictatorial tone, I waive it in deference to an old friend whose heart I have always supposed to be right.

"As to the policy I seem to be pursuing, as you say, I have not meant to leave any one in doubt. I would save the Union. I would save it in the shortest way under the Constitution.

"The sooner the national authority can be restored, the nearer the Union will be the Union as it was.

"If there be those who would not save the Union unless they could at the same time save slavery, I do not agree with them.

"If there be those who would not save the Union unless they could at the same time destroy slavery, I do not agree with them.

"*My paramount object is to save the Union, and not either to save or destroy slavery.*

"If I could save the Union without freeing any slave, I would do it; if I could save it by freeing all the slaves, I would do it; and if I could do it by freeing some, and leaving others alone, I would also do that.

"What I do about slavery and the colored race, I do because I believe it helps to saves this Union; and what I forbear, I forbear because I do not believe it would help to save the Union.

"I shall do less whenever I shall believe what I am doing hurts the cause, and I shall do more when I believe doing more will help the cause.

"I shall try to correct errors when shown to be errors, and I shall adopt new views so fast as they shall appear to be true views.

"I have here stated my purpose according to my views of official duty; and I intend no modification of my oft-expressed personal wish, that all men everywhere could be free. "Yours,

"A. LINCOLN."

Here, again, we see the wisdom of the serpent, and the harmlessness of the dove, in the letter which shows him ready to follow the path of duty whenever clearly seen, and that was all the men of any party could rightfully ask.

When he could consistently plead for emancipation, how earnest and outspoken were his words! In his Annual Message he said, "We cannot escape history. We of this Congress and this Administration will be remembered in spite of ourselves. . . . We say we are for the Union. The world will not forget that we say this. We know how to save the Union. The world knows we know how to save it. We, even we here, hold the power, and bear the responsibility. In giving freedom to the slave, we assure freedom to the free, — honorable alike in what we give and what we preserve. We shall nobly save or meanly lose the last best hope of earth. Other means may succeed: this could not, cannot fail. The way is plain, peaceful, generous, just, — a way which, if followed, the world will forever applaud, and God must forever bless."

The noble author of a glorious proclamation never retracted it, never changed his views concerning it. In a letter written in August, 1863, he said, referring to the peace that he expected, but hardly lived to see, "And then there will be some black men who can remember that with silent tongue, and clinched teeth, and steady eye, and well-poised bayonet, they have helped mankind on to this great consummation; while I fear that there will be some white men unable to forget, that, with malignant heart and deceitful speech, they have striven to hinder it."

In his Annual Message, December, 1863, he referred to the success which had attended the proclamation of emancipation, and added, "While I remain in my present position, I shall not attempt to retract or modify the Emancipation Proclamation; nor shall I return to slavery any person who is free by the terms of that proclamation, or by any of the acts of Congress."

More and more clearly will it be seen, as time rolls on, that the President could not have done his duty, and yet have failed to free the slave.

"From the first cannon-shot, it was plain that the Rebellion was nothing but slavery in arms; but such was the power of slavery, even in the free States, that months elapsed before this giant criminal was directly attacked. Generals in the field were tender with regard to it, as if it were a church, or a work of the fine arts. It was only under the teaching of disaster that the country was aroused. The first step was taken in Congress after the defeat at Bull Run. But still the President hesitated. Disaster thickened and graves opened, until, at last, the country saw that only by justice could we hope for divine favor; and the President, who leaned so closely upon the popular heart, pronounced that great word by which all slaves in the rebel States were set free. Let it be named forever to his glory, that he grasped the thunderbolt, even though tardily, under which the Rebellion staggered to its fall; that, following up the blow, he enlisted colored citizens as soldiers in the national army; and that he declared his final purpose never to retract or modify the Emancipation Proclamation, nor to return into slavery any person free by the terms of that instrument, or by any of the acts of Congress, saying loftily, 'If the people should, by whatever mode or means, make it an executive duty to re-enslave such persons, another, and not I, must be the instrument to perform it.'

"It was sometimes said that the proclamation was of doubtful constitutionality. If this criticism did not proceed from sympathy with slavery, it evidently proceeded from the prevailing superstition with regard to this idol. Future jurists will read with astonishment that once a flagrant wrong could be considered at any time as having any rights which a court was bound to respect, and especially that rebels in arms could be considered as having any title to the services of people whose allegiance was primarily due to the United States. But, turning from these conclusions, it seems to be plain, that slavery, which stood exclusively on local law, without any support in natural law, must have fallen with the local government, both legally and constitutionally : *legally*, inasmuch as it ceased to have any valid legal support ; and *constitutionally*, inasmuch as it came at once within the exclusive jurisdiction of the Constitution, where liberty is the prevailing law. The President did not act upon these principles ; but, speaking with the voice of authority, he said, 'Let the slaves be free!' What Court and Congress hesitated to declare, he proclaimed, and thus enrolled himself among the world's emancipators." *

Little did that gentle mother, long vanished from her dear son's earthly path, imagine, when she so desired that he should learn to read and write, that his pen would ever trace such life-giving, joy-inspiring words. Glad hearts

* Hon. Charles Sumner.

everywhere among true men and women welcomed the glorious decree. The pencil of the artist * and the pen of the poet † vied in commemorating the event, and expressing their exultant joy; and human eloquence is powerless to express the blissful gratitude with which it was received by the long-oppressed race whom it lifted from the degradation of slavery to the glorious heights of freedom.

No document can tower above the last mentioned; for its altitude will remain unsurpassed, till, in the fulness of God's time, the chains of sin shall be broken, evil shall be overcome with good, and the proclamation of universal freedom from sin and sorrow shall be uttered in the words, "The kingdoms of this world have become the kingdoms of our Lord and of his Christ," and "God shall be all and in all."

This chapter may fittingly close with a document, than which none more chaste and beautiful in style can be found. It is a proclamation for a day of thanksgiving. One has already been given which proclaimed a day of fasting. A proclamation, recommending that the people in-

* W. T. Carleton of Boston painted an exquisite picture, entitled "Waiting for the Hour," depicting their anxiety who waited for the time when the chains would fall as the proclamation came in force on the first day of January, 1863. This picture was afterward presented to President Lincoln.

† Among other hearty tributes to the President was one entitled "God bless Abraham Lincoln!" It was written by Mrs. Caroline A. Mason, whose touching song, "Do they miss me at home?" has been sung by Union soldiers with tearful eyes beside many a camp-fire and in many a hospital. Her poem closes thus: —

"*God bless him:* can we more? In this,
The perfectness of human bliss,
All joy, all peace, all fulness is.

And so God bless him! Once again
Take up the burden, voice and pen,
While all the people say, 'Amen!'"

formally assemble and thank God for victories in East Tennessee, was issued in December, 1863. One to which allusion is here specially made was as follows: —

"It has pleased Almighty God to hearken to the supplications and prayers of an afflicted people, and to vouchsafe to the army and the navy of the United States, on the land and on the sea, victories so signal and so effective as to furnish reasonable grounds for augmented confidence that the union of these States will be maintained, their constitutions preserved, and their peace and prosperity permanently preserved.

"But these victories have been accorded not without sacrifice of life, limb, and liberty, incurred by the brave, patriotic, and loyal citizens. Domestic affliction in every part of the country follows in the train of these fearful bereavements. It is meet and right to recognize and confess the presence of the Almighty Father, and the power of his hand, equally in these triumphs and these sorrows.

"Now, therefore, be it known that I do set apart Thursday, the sixth day of August next, to be observed as a day for national thanksgiving, praise, and prayer: and I invite the people of the United States to assemble on that occasion in their customary places of worship, and, in the forms approved by their own conscience, render the homage due to the Divine Majesty for the wonderful things he has done in the nation's behalf, and invoke the influence of his Holy Spirit to subdue the anger which has produced and so long sustained a needless and cruel rebellion; to change the hearts of the insurgents; to guide the counsels of the Government with wisdom adequate to so great a national emergency; and to visit with tender care and consolation, throughout the length and breadth of our land, all those who, through the vicissitudes of marches, voyages, battles, and sieges, have been brought to suffer in mind, body, or estate, and family; to lead the whole nation through paths of repentance, and submission to the Divine Will, back to the perfect enjoyment of union and fraternal peace.

"In witness whereof, I have hereunto set my hand, and caused the seal of the United States to be affixed.

"Done at the city of Washington, this 15th day of July, in the year of our Lord one thousand eight hundred and sixty-three, and of the independence of the United States of America the eighty-eighth.

"ABRAHAM LINCOLN.

"By the President:

"WILLIAM H. SEWARD, *Secretary of State.*"

The documents contained in this chapter form a part of our national history, which no true American will ever ponder but with pride and satisfaction. All of them had immediate results that were glorious and salutary; and one at least of them will exert an influence grand and far-reaching as the march of Time, like to the echo of God's voice of promise and hope amid the bowers of Eden, which will extend till the answering anthem of a redeemed world and a rejoicing universe shall rise "to Him that sitteth upon the throne, and to the Lamb for ever."

CHAPTER IX.

ANECDOTES.

"Thereby hangs a tale." — SHAKSPEARE.

"A word fitly spoken is like apples of gold in pictures of silver." — PROV. xxv. 2.

THERE is a time to laugh, as well as a time to weep, if we may credit the wise man; and, of the two, the smile is to be preferred to the tear, since it will help to send more sunshine abroad in a world where needed spiritual discipline, in consequence of sin, must bring many shadows. Jacob Abbott has taught his thousands of readers that "cheerfulness is a duty;" and one may well suspect the long face of covering a bad heart. "Other things being equal," the truest Christian is the most cheerful one; and that man or woman is highly favored who has received that inheritance of mirthfulness which enables him without effort to "look on the bright side."

President Lincoln was far from being a mirthful man, in one sense; overflowing with fun and jollity. He had borne too many burdens not to have lost some elasticity of spirit; and the natural buoyancy of youth was, as we know, early lessened by the loss of his almost idolized mother. Moreover, later life had brought those peculiar trials we have mentioned; and one would hardly expect to see in President Lincoln the sportive, careless, mirthful Donatello whom Hawthorne pictured ere he passed away.* Nor would we like to see the restless buoyancy of excessive animal spirits in one occupying the position of the nation's head.

* "Marble Faun."

President Lincoln had the happy medium. He was cheerful without levity, as he was ofttimes sad without being misanthropic. Emerson says of him, "His broad good humor, running easily into jocular talk, in which he delighted, and in which he excelled, was a rich gift to this wise man. It enabled him to keep his secret; to meet every kind of man, and every rank in society; to take off the edge of the severest decisions; to mask his own purpose, and sound his companion, and to catch with true instinct the temper of every company he addressed. And, more than all, it is to a man of severe labor, in anxious and exhausting crises, the natural restorative, good as sleep, and is the protection of the over-driven brain against rancor and insanity.

"He is the author of a multitude of good sayings, so disguised as pleasantries, that it is certain they had no reputation at first but as jests; and only later, by the very acceptance and adoption they find in the mouths of millions, turn out to be the wisdom of the hour. I am sure, if this man had ruled in a period of less facility of printing, he would have become mythological in a very few years, like Æsop or Pilpay, or one of the Seven Wise Masters, by his fables and proverbs."

His cheerfulness of demeanor, and speech, sometimes led strangers into an error in regard to him. They thought him too careless of the dignity which belonged to his position; but they could not say he neglected the "weightier matters of the law," even if he did sometimes seem to omit the "tithes of mint, anise, and cumin."

One who knew him well* thus renders testimony to the excellence of his character even in these particulars:—

* Col. Deming.

"He was not over-careful of his dignity, feeling assured that his dignity would take care of itself; and consenting to rend the web of official formalities, and to waive all ceremony and precedence which might bar his passage to a good deed by the most expeditious route. He has been convicted, in contempt of 'the divinity which doth hedge a king,' of conferring with his counsellors in a great emergency, and of performing an act of kindness and mercy, enveloped in no robe of state but a cotton night-gown of scanty proportions; and on one memorable occasion he even presumed to solve an enigma, raised in a congress of ambassadors, by the little story of 'root, hog, or die.' He was what Dr. Johnson calls a thoroughly 'clubbable' man; eminently social and familiar; in private interviews, and sometimes in public, overflowing with illustrations of every theme; always apt and racy, and frequently humorous, with a habit, like the doctor himself, of upsetting a pedantry or a sophism by an epigram or an anecdote, and with a story-telling method of reasoning like our own Dr. Franklin. While unrivalled as a *raconteur* in the pith and variety of his store, he was not half so broad in his narrations as many an unassuming Chesterfield on both sides of the water. ... I can adopt and indorse the precise language of Mr. F. B. Carpenter, who, as an artist, had free access to Mr. Lincoln's presence, and was for several months an inmate of the White House, when he says, 'I feel that it is due to Mr. Lincoln's memory to state, that during my residence in Washington, after witnessing his intercourse with all classes of people, including governors, senators, members of Congress, officers of the army, and familiar friends, I cannot recollect to have heard him relate a circumstance to any one of them all that would have been out of place if uttered in a lady's drawing-room.'"

The same gentleman speaks of an interview which he had with the President just after Gen. Frémont had declined to run against him for the presidency; and says, "The magnificent Bible which the negroes of Washington had just presented him lay upon the table; and, while we were both examining it, I recited the somewhat remarkable passage from the Chronicles, 'Eastward were six Levites, northward four a day, southward four a day, and towards Assuppim two and two, at Parbar westward, four at the causeway, and two at Parbar.' He immediately challenged me to find any such passage as that in *his* Bible. After I had pointed it out to him, and he was satisfied of its genuineness, he asked me if I remembered the text which his friends had recently applied to Frémont; and instantly turned to a verse in the First of Samuel, put on his spectacles, and read, in his slow, peculiar, and waggish tone, 'And every one that was in distress, and every one that was in debt, and every one that was discontented, gathered themselves unto him; and he became a captain over them: and there were with him about four hundred men.' "

Here is a story which has been "going the rounds" of the press, entitled —

"LINCOLN'S FIRST DOLLAR." — One evening, in the Executive Chamber, there were present a number of gentlemen, among them Mr. Seward.

"A point in the conversation suggesting the thought, Mr. Lincoln said, 'Seward, you never heard, did you, how I earned my first dollar?' — 'No,' said Mr. Seward. 'Well,' replied he, 'I was about eighteen years of age. I belonged, you know, to what they call down South "the scrubs:" people who do not own land and slaves are nobody there. But we had succeeded in raising, chiefly by my labor, sufficient produce, as I thought, to justify me in taking it down the river to sell.

"'After much persuasion, I got the consent of mother to go, and constructed a little flat-boat large enough to take the barrel or two of things that we had gathered, with myself and little bundle, down to New Orleans. A steamer was coming down the river. We have, you know, no wharves on the Western streams; and the custom was, if passengers were at any of the landings, for them to go out in a boat, the steamer stopping, and taking them on board.

"'I was contemplating my new flat-boat, and wondering whether I could make it stronger or improve it in any particular, when two men came down to the shore in carriages with trunks, and, looking at the different boats, singled out mine, and asked, "Who owns this?" I answered, somewhat modestly, "I do."—"Will you," said one of them, "take us and our trunks out to the steamer?"—"Certainly," said I. I was very glad to have the chance of earning something. I supposed that each would give me two or three bits. The trunks were put on my flat-boat, the passengers seated themselves on the trunks, and I sculled them out to the steamboat.

"'They got on board, and I lifted up their heavy trunks, and put them on the deck. The steamer was about to put on steam again, when I called out that they had forgotten to pay me. Each of them took from his pocket a silver half-dollar, and threw it on the floor of the boat. I could scarcely believe my eyes as I picked up the money. Gentlemen, you may think it was a very little thing, and in these days it seems like a trifle; but it was a most important incident in my life. I could scarcely credit that I, a poor boy, had earned a dollar in less than a day,—that by honest work I had earned a dollar. The world seemed brighter and fairer before me.

I was a more hopeful and confident being from that time.' "

Carleton,* the favorite correspondent of the "Boston Journal," narrated to the writer the following anecdote concerning one of the President's humorous remarks: It was during the week before Richmond was taken. The President was with Gen. Grant and others at City-Point headquarters. The party sat where they could see the river. A flat-boat made its appearance, with apparently a large family on board. The President was informed that it was a planter of the vicinity, with his wife and legitimate children, and not a few colored women with their children, which were also supposed to be his own. "Ah! yes," said the President, "I see. It is Abraham, Isaac, and Ishmael, all in one boat." The aptness of the Scripture allusion, and the quickness of the President in responding, woke a smile on every countenance.

The Hon. Charles Sumner, in his eulogy, thus refers to the humor of the President: "His humor has also become a proverb. He insisted sometimes that he had no invention, but only a memory. He did not forget the good things which he heard, and was never without a familiar story to illustrate his meaning. When he spoke, the recent West seemed to vie with the ancient East in apologue and fable."

A writer in "Harpers' Monthly" gives several anecdotes concerning the President, with whom he seems to have been intimately acquainted. One of them is as follows: "Mr. Lincoln visited the Army of the Potomac in the spring of 1863, and, free from the annoyances of office, was considerably refreshed and rested; but even there the mental anxieties which never forsook him seemed to cast him down at times with a great weight.

* C. C. Coffin, Esq.

We left Washington late in the afternoon; and, a snow-storm soon after coming on, the steamer was anchored, for the night, off Indian Head, on the Maryland shore of the Potomac. The President left the little knot in the cabin, and, sitting alone in a corner, seemed absorbed in the saddest reflections for a time; then, beckoning a companion to him, said, 'What will you wager that half our iron-clads are at the bottom of Charleston Harbor?' This being the first intimation which the other had of Dupont's attack, which was then begun, he hesitated to reply; when the President added, 'The people will expect big things when they hear of this; but it is too late, —*too late!*'

"During that little voyage, the captain of the steamer, a frank, modest old sailor, was so much affected by the careworn appearance of the President, that he came to the writer, and confessed that he had received the same impression of the Chief Magistrate that many had. Hearing of his 'little stories' and his humor, he had supposed him to have no cares or sadness; but a sight of that anxious and sad face had undeceived him, and he wanted to tell the President how much he had unintentionally wronged him, feeling that he had committed upon him a personal wrong. The captain was duly introduced to the President, who talked with him privately for a space, being touched as well as amused at what he called 'Capt. M——'s freeing his mind.'

"An amusing yet touching instance of the President's pre-occupation of mind occurred at one of his levees, when he was shaking hands with a host of visitors passing him in a continuous stream. An intimate acquaintance received the usual conventional hand-shake and salutation, but, perceiving that he was not recognized, kept his ground, instead of moving on, and spoke again; when the President, roused by a dim consciousness that something unusual had happened, perceived who stood before him, and, seizing his friend's hand, shook it again heartily, saying, 'How do you do? how do you do? Excuse me for not noticing you at first: the fact is, I was thinking of a man down South.' He afterwards privately acknowledged that the 'man down South' was Sherman, then on his march to the sea.

"Mr. Lincoln had not a hopeful temperament, and, though he looked at the bright side of things, was always prepared for disaster and defeat. With his wonderful faculty for discerning results, he often saw success where others saw disaster, but oftener perceived a failure when others were elated with victory, or were temporarily deceived by appearances. Of a great cavalry raid, which filled the newspapers with glowing exultation, but failed to cut the communications which it had been designed to destroy, he briefly said, 'That was good circus-riding: it will do to fill a column in the newspapers; but I don't see that it has brought any thing else to pass.' He often said that the worst feature about newspapers was that they were so sure to be 'ahead of the hounds,' outrunning events, and exciting expectations which were sure to be disappointed. One of the worst effects of a victory, he said, was to lead people to expect that the war was about over in consequence of it; but he was never weary of commending the patience of the American people, which he thought something matchless and touching. . . .

"The world will never hear the last of the 'little stories' with which the President garnished or illustrated his conversation and his early stump-speeches. He said, however, that, as near as he could reckon, about one-sixth of those which were credited to him were old accquaintances: all of the rest were the productions of other and better story-tellers than himself. Said he, 'I do generally remember a good story when I hear it; but I never did invent any thing original: I am only a retail-dealer.' His anecdotes were seldom told for the sake of the telling, but because they fitted in just where they came, and shed a light on the argument that nothing else could. He was not witty, but brimful of humor; and, though he was quick to appreciate a good pun, I never knew of his making but one, which was on the Christian name of a friend, to whom he said, 'You have yet to be elected to the place I hold; but Noah's *reign* was before Abraham.' He thought the chief characteristic of American humor was its grotesqueness and extravagance; and the story of the man who was so tall that he was 'laid out' in a rope-walk, the soprano voice so high that it had to be climbed over by a ladder, and the Dutchman's expression of 'somebody tying his dog loose,' all made a permanent lodgement in his mind. . . .

"People were sometimes disappointed because he appeared before them with a written speech. The best explanation of that habit of his was his remark to a friend, who noticed a roll of manuscript in the hand of the President as he came into the parlor, while waiting for the serenade which was given him on the night following his re-election. Said he, 'I know what you're thinking about; but there's no clap-trap about me; and I am free to say, that, in the excitement of the moment, I am sure to say something which I am sorry for when I see it in print: so I have it here in black and white, and there are no mistakes made. People attach too much importance to what I say anyhow.'

"Upon another occasion, hearing that I was in the parlor, he sent for me to come up into the library, where

I found him writing on a piece of common stiff box-board with a pencil. Said he, after he had finished, 'Here is one speech of mine which has never been printed, and I think it worth printing. Just see what you think.' He then read the following, which is copied *verbatim* from the familiar handwriting before me: —

"'On Thursday of last week two ladies from Tennessee came before the President, asking the release of their husbands, held as prisoners of war at Johnson's Island. They were put off until Friday; when they came again, and were again put off until Saturday. At each of the interviews, one of the ladies urged that her husband was a religious man. On Saturday, when the President ordered the release of the prisoners, he said to this lady, "You say your husband is a religious man: tell him, when you meet him, that I say I am not much a judge of religion, but that, in my opinion, that religion that sets men to rebel and fight against their Government, because, as they think, that Government does not sufficiently help *some* men to eat their bread in the sweat of *other* men's faces, is not the sort of religion upon which people can get to heaven."'

"To this the President signed his name at my request, by way of joke, and added for a caption, 'The President's last, shortest, and best speech;' under which title it was duly published in one of the Washington newspapers. His message to the last session of Congress was first written upon the same sort of white pasteboard above referred to; its stiffness enabling him to lay it on his knee as he sat easily in his arm-chair, writing and erasing as he thought and wrought out his idea."

The author of the "Pioneer Boy" says of Mr. Lincoln, "He never felt above his business. He was never ashamed of his origin or his poverty. When consulted with regard to the incidents of his early life, he remarked, 'You can find the whole of my early life in a single line of Gray's Elegy, —

> 'The short and simple annals of the poor.' "

Carpenter, the artist, has contributed to the "New-York Independent" several chapters of reminiscences of Mr. Lincoln, from which the following is taken: —

SHAKSPEARE. — Something was said about the play of "Hamlet." Mr. Lincoln waked up with the mention of the theme, and soon after said, — and I have often thought of his words with a sad interest since his own assassination, — "There is one passage of the play of 'Hamlet' which is very apt to be slurred over by the actor, or omitted altogether, which seems to me the choicest part of the play. It is," he went on to say, "the soliloquy of the king after the murder. It always struck me as one of the finest touches of nature in the world." . . .

Remaining in thought for a few moments, he continued: —

"The opening of the play of 'King Richard the Third' seems to me often entirely misapprehended. It is quite common for an actor to come upon the stage, and, in a sophomorical style, to begin with a flourish: —

> 'Now is the winter of our discontent
> Made glorious summer by this sun of York,
> And all the clouds that lowered upon our house
> In the deep bosom of the ocean buried.'

Now," said he, "this is all wrong. Richard, you remember, had been, and was then, plotting the destruction of his brothers, to make room for himself. Outwardly the most loyal to the newly crowned king, secretly he could scarcely contain his impatience at the obstacles still in the way of his own elevation. He appears upon the stage, just after the crowning of Edward, burning with repressed hate and jealousy. The prologue is the utterance of the most intense bitterness and satire."

Then, unconsciously assuming the character, Mr. Lincoln repeated, also from memory, Richard's soliloquy, rendering it with a degree of force and power that made it seem like a new creation to me. Though familiar with the passage from boyhood, I can truly say that never till that moment had I fully appreciated its spirit. I could not refrain from laying down my palette and brushes, and applauding the President heartily upon his conclusion, saying at the same time, half in earnest, that "I was not sure but that he had made a mistake in the choice of a profession," considerably, as may be imagined, to his amusement.

A Presidential Message.—It will be remembered that an extra session of Congress was called in July following Mr. Lincoln's inauguration. In the message then sent in, speaking of secession, and the measures taken by the Southern leaders to bring it about, there occurs the following remark: "With rebellion thus sugar-coated, they have been drugging the public mind of their section for more than thirty years, until at length they have brought many good men to a willingness to take up arms against the Government," &c. Mr. De Frees, the Government printer, told me, that, when the message was being printed, he was a good deal disturbed by the use of the term "sugar-coated," and finally went to the President about it. Their relations to each other being of the most intimate character, he told Mr. Lincoln frankly that he ought to remember that a message to Congress was a different affair from a speech at a mass-meeting in Illinois; that the messages became a part of history, and should be written accordingly.

"What is the matter now?" inquired the President.

"Why," said Mr. De Frees, "you have used an undignified expression in the message;" and then, reading the paragraph aloud, he added, "I would alter the structure of that if I were you."

"De Frees," replied Mr. Lincoln, "that word expresses precisely my idea, and I am not going to change it. The time will never come in this country when the people won't know exactly what *sugar-coated* means!"

The following anecdote was related by President Lincoln with great effect, and proves that he well understood the deadly nature of the great conflict to come:—

"'I once knew,' he said, 'a good sound churchman, whom we will call Brown, who was in a committee to erect a bridge over a very dangerous and rapid river. Architect after architect failed; and, at last, Brown said he had a friend named Jones, who had built several bridges, and could build this. "Let us have him in," said the committee. In came Jones. "Can you build this bridge, sir?"—"Yes," replied Jones, "I could build a bridge to the infernal regions if necessary." The sober committee were horrified. But, when Jones retired, Brown thought it but fair to defend his friend. "I know Jones so well," said he, "he is so honest a man, and so good an architect, that, if he states soberly and positively that he can build a bridge to Hades, why, I believe it; but I have my doubts about the abutment on the infernal side." So,' Mr. Lincoln added, 'when politicians said they could harmonize the Northern and Southern wings of the democracy, why, I believed them; but I had my doubts about the abutment on the Southern side.'"*

* Rev. John S. C. Abbott's "History of the Civil War."

The following is a characteristic short sermon, which, it is stated, President Lincoln was in the habit of preaching to his children: —

"Don't drink, don't smoke, don't chew, don't swear, don't gamble, don't lie, don't cheat; love your fellow-men as well as God; love truth, love virtue, and be happy!"

CHAPTER X.

CHRISTIAN WORDS AND DEEDS.

"Be good, sweet friend, and let who will be clever;
Do noble deeds, not dream them all day long;
And so make life, death, and that vast Forever,
One grand, sweet song."
REV. CHARLES KINGSLEY.

"The law of truth was in his mouth, and iniquity was not found in his lips." —
MALACHI ii. 6.

ABRAHAM LINCOLN was a Christian; but no particular branch of Zion can claim him. He belongs to that universal Church of which Christ alone is head, and all whose members are imbued with their Master's spirit. Under different names, or perhaps, like him, with no denominational rank at all, the great souls that delight to do good, and desire to live and act for the honor of God, are moving forward at the command of one Leader, and to one grand destiny. These are the world's workers. Imbued with Christ's spirit of self-sacrificing love, they act as if, like him, they came to earth, "not to be ministered unto, but to minister." And who shall deny them a place amid God's elect, or shut against them at last the door of heaven? It is not so much creed as life that is to be weighed in the unerring scales of God's justice. A man may profess to have a pure and noble creed, but in daily deeds contradict it; and a man may have a warped and narrow view of truth, and yet his life be broader and better than his creed. But, generally, "as a man thinketh, so is he." Men are biassed by their religious views and opinions; and he who has profoundest faith in things unseen is most likely to labor assiduously in doing God's will amid the things that are seen and temporal.

Thus did our martyred President. He never joined a church, because, as he said, he found difficulty in giving his assent, without mental reservation, to the long complicated statements of Christian doctrine which characterize their Articles of Belief, and Confessions of Faith.

"When any church," he continued, "will inscribe over its altar, as its sole qualification for membership, the Saviour's condensed statement of the substance of both law and gospel, 'Thou shalt love the Lord thy God with all thy heart, and with all thy soul, and with all thy mind, and thy neighbor as thyself,' that church will I join with all my heart and all my soul."

The President was a great reader of the Bible. The last photograph taken of him represents him reading that blessed volume, with little Thaddeus standing at his side.

Rev. W. M. Thayer says of him in his youth, "For a boy of his age, he was excelled by few in his acquaintance with the Scriptures. The Bible, catechism, and the old spelling-book named, being the only books in the family at this time, and there being no papers, either religious or secular, the Bible was read much more than it would have been if other volumes had been possessed. . . . That same Bible is still in the possession of a relative in the State of Illinois." *

As long as he lived, the President valued the Best of Books. One who knew him intimately says, "The Bible was a very familiar study with the President; whole

* "Pioneer Boy," p. 58.

chapters of Isaiah, the New Testament, and the Psalms, being fixed in his memory: and he would sometimes correct a misquotation of Scripture, giving generally the chapter and verse where it could be found. He liked the Old Testament best, and dwelt on the simple beauty of the historical books. Once, speaking of his own age and strength, he quoted with admiration that passage, 'His eye was not dim, nor his natural force abated.' I do not know that he thought then, how, like that Moses of old, he was to stand on Pisgah, and see a peaceful land which he was not to enter." * It has been said that the President was in the habit of rising early, and spending an hour in the reading of the Scriptures, and prayer. It would be well if all in authority would imitate an example so good and salutary: then might we hope that our nation would speedily become "one whose God is the Lord," and be evermore a "praise in the earth." †

Shaping his life-course by the chart, which, emanating from God himself, cannot be imperfect, the President was always a temperate man.

"Through his whole life he remained the advocate of temperance. He regretted the intemperance that existed in the army. In reply to a delegation of the Sons

* "Harpers' Monthly," July, 1865.

† Like Daniel Webster, Byron, and other writers, Lincoln drew largely on the Bible for illustration. He said to a friend, that "many years ago, when the custom of lecture-giving was more common than since, he was induced to try his hand at composing a literary lecture, — something which he thought entirely out of his line. The subject, he said, was not defined; but his purpose was to analyze inventions and discoveries, "to get at the bottom of things," and to show when, where, how, and why such things were invented or discovered; and, so far as possible, to find where the first mention is made of some uncommon things. *The Bible, he said, he found to be the richest storehouse for such knowledge;* and he then gave one or two illustrations which were new to his hearers. The lecture was never finished, and was left among his loose papers at Springfield when he came to Washington." *

* "Harpers' Monthly."

of Temperance on this subject, he said, in substance, that "when he was a young man, long ago, before the Sons of Temperance, as an organization, had an existence, he, in a humble way, made temperance speeches; and he thought he might say, that, to this day, he had never, by his example, belied what he then said. As to the suggestions for the purpose of the advancement of the cause of temperance in the army, he could not respond to them. To prevent intemperance in the army is the aim of a great part of the rules and articles of war. It is a part of the law of the land, and was so, he presumed, long ago, to dismiss officers for drunkenness. He was not sure, that, consistently with the public service, more could be done than has been done. All, therefore, he could promise, was to have a copy of the address submitted to the principal departments, and have it considered whether it contains any suggestions which will improve the cause of temperance and repress drunkenness in the army any better than is already done. He thought the reasonable men of the world have long since agreed that drunkenness is one of the greatest, if not the very greatest, of all evils among mankind. That is not a matter of dispute. All men agree that intemperance is a great curse, but differ about the cure." *

One more extract only from Mr. Thayer's testimonial to the great and good man. He says that a friend of Mr. Lincoln, who had known him as a neighbor for many years, writes thus to him: "I have known him long and well; and I can say in truth, I think (take him altogether) he is the best man I ever saw. Although he has never made a public profession of religion, I nevertheless believe that he has the fear of God before his eyes, and that he goes daily to a throne of grace, and asks wisdom, light,

* "President's Words," p. 163.

and knowledge to enable him faithfully to discharge his duties."

Bishop Simpson thus testifies of the departed Chief Magistrate: "Abraham Lincoln was a good man. He was known as an honest, temperate, forgiving man; a just man; a man of noble heart in every way. . . .

"As a ruler, I doubt if any President has ever shown such trust in God, or, in public documents, so frequently referred to divine aid. Often did he remark to friends and to delegations, that his hope for our success rested in his conviction that God would bless our efforts because we were trying to do right. To the address of a large religious body, he replied, 'Thanks be unto God, who, in our national trials, giveth us the churches.' To a minister, who said he hoped the Lord was on our side, he replied that it gave him no concern whether the Lord was on our side or not: 'For,' he added, 'I know the Lord is always on the side of right;' and with deep feeling added, 'But God is my witness that it is my constant anxiety and prayer that both myself and this nation should be on the Lord's side.'"

The following incident must not be omitted in this mention of the President's Christian words and deeds. During the visit of Mr. Lincoln to New York in 1860, he visited a mission-school at the Five-Points' House of Industry. The teacher thus narrates the circumstance:—

"Our Sunday school in the Five Points was assembled one Sabbath morning, when I noticed a tall, remarkable-looking man enter the room, and take a seat among us. He listened with fixed attention to our exercises; and his countenance expressed such genuine interest, that I approached him, and suggested that he might be willing to say something to the children. He accepted the invitation with evident pleasure; and, coming forward, began a simple address, which at once fascinated every little hearer, and hushed the room into silence. His language was strikingly beautiful, and his tones musical with intensest feeling. The little faces around him would droop into sad conviction as he uttered sentences of warning, and would lighten into sunshine as he spoke cheerful words of promise. Once or twice he attempted to close his remarks; but the imperative shout of 'Go on! oh, do go on!' would compel him to resume. As I looked upon the gaunt and sinewy frame of the stranger, and marked his powerful head and determined features, now touched into softness by the impressions of the moment, I felt an irrepressible curiosity to learn something more about him; and when he was quietly leaving the room, I begged to know his name. He courteously replied, 'It is Abraham Lincoln, from Illinois.'"

Thus did the future President spend a portion of his Sabbath, while absent from his home, in a distant city; and thus, in doing and getting good, would he have others keep the Sabbath. His deep and earnest reverence for Christianity is seen in the following official paper, issued on the 16th of November, 1862: —

"The President, Commander-in-chief of the Army and Navy, desires and enjoins the orderly observance of the Sabbath by the officers and men in the military and naval service. The importance for man and beast of the prescribed weekly rest, the sacred rights of Christian soldiers and sailors, a becoming deference to the best sentiment of a Christian people, and a due regard for the divine will, demand that Sunday labor in the army and navy be reduced to the measure of strict necessity.

"The discipline and character of the national forces should not suffer, nor the cause they defend be imperilled, by the profanation of the day or name of the Most High.

'At this time of public distress,' adopting the woids of Washington in 1776, 'men may find enough to do in the service of God and their country, without abandoning themselves to vice and immorality.' The first general order issued by the Father of his Country after the Declaration of Independence indicates the spirit in which our institutions were founded, and should ever be defended: 'The General hopes and trusts that every officer and man will endeavor to live and act as becomes a Christian soldier defending the dearest rights and liberties of his country.'

"ABRAHAM LINCOLN."

Among the kindly and appreciative words of the amiable President may be found his brief speech on the 18th March, 1864, at the close of the successful fair held in the Patent Office in Washington. It was as follows:—

"LADIES AND GENTLEMEN,—I appear to say but a word. This extraordinary war in which we are engaged falls heavily upon all classes of people, but the most heavily upon the soldier. For it has been said, all that a man hath will he give for his life; and, while all contribute of their substance, the soldier puts his life at stake, and often yields it up in his country's cause. The highest merit, then, is due to the soldier.

"In this extraordinary war, extraordinary developments have manifested themselves, such as have not been seen in former wars; and, among these manifestations, nothing has been more remarkable than these fairs for the relief of suffering soldiers and their families. And the chief agents in these fairs are the women of America. I am not accustomed to the use of the language of eulogy; I have never studied the art of paying compliments to women: but I must say, that if all that has been said by orators and poets, since the creation of the world, in praise of women, were applied to the women of America, it would not do them justice for their conduct during this war. I will close by saying, God bless the women of America!"

Again: just before he wrote the immortal proclamation, he said, "Do not misunderstand me: . . . I have not decided against a proclamation of liberty to the slaves, but hold the matter under advisement. And I can assure you that the subject is on my mind, by day and night, more than any other. Whatever shall appear to be God's will, I will do." *

And yet again: in words of living faith he says, "If we have patience, if we restrain ourselves, if we allow ourselves not to run off in a passion, I still have confidence that the Almighty, the Maker of the universe, will, through the instrumentality of this great and intelligent people, bring us through this, as he has through all the other difficulties of our country." † This was said in 1861. In 1864, the President's faith was lost in sight.

See the modesty of our late President in his own record of his life, furnished for a "Dictionary of Congress."

"Born Feb. 12, 1809, in Hardin County, Ky.

"Education defective.

"Profession, a lawyer. Have been a captain of volunteers in the Black-Hawk War.

"Postmaster at a very small office. Four times a member of the Illinois Legislature, and was a member of the lower house of Congress.

"Yours, &c., "A. LINCOLN."

Here is the record of an act of kindness, from the pen of a Western editor: —

* "President's Words," p. 118. † Ibid.

"I dropped in upon Mr. Lincoln on Monday last, and found him busily engaged in counting green-backs. 'This, sir,' said he, 'is something out of my usual line: but a President of the United States has a multiplicity of duties not specified in the Constitution, or Acts of Congress; this is one of them. This money belongs to a poor negro, who is a porter in one of the departments (the Treasury), and who is at present very sick with the small-pox. He is now in the hospital, and could not draw his pay because he could not sign his name. I have been at considerable trouble to overcome the difficulty, and get it for him; and have at length succeeded in cutting red tape, as you newspaper-men say. I am now dividing the money, and putting by a portion, labelled in an envelope with my own hands, according to his wish." *

An English clergyman said in his eulogy, "One or two illustrations of his personal kindness have just come to my knowledge through a friend who has recently returned from the United States. This gentleman told me that he was one day conversing with the general in command of one of the armies, on the subject of desertion; when the general said, 'The first week of my command, there were twenty-four deserters sentenced by court-martial to be shot; and the warrants for their execution were sent to the President to be signed: he refused. I went to Washington, and had an interview. I said, 'Mr. President, unless these men are made an example of, the army itself is in danger. Mercy to the few is cruelty to the many.' He replied, 'Mr. General, there are already too many weeping widows in the United States. For God's sake, don't ask me to add to the number; for I

* "Chicago Tribune."

won't do it.' A young sentry was found asleep on his post: he was sentenced to be shot; but the President came into camp, and granted the earnest petition of the lad. The dead body of that youth was afterwards found among the slain on the field of Fredericksburg; and under his waistcoat, next to his breast, was a photograph of the President, beneath which the lad had written, 'God bless President Lincoln!' Many similar incidents might be cited to show how tender-hearted he was, and how deeply he was beloved by multitudes who have received from him personal marks of kindness." *

At the time when the young soldier above mentioned was under sentence of death, "Carleton" (C. C. Coffin), of the "Journal," was in Washington. He became convinced that the case was one deserving pardon; that the young man had been kept awake too long, and was not desirous of failing in duty, but was absolutely overpowered by fatigue. On the evening preceding the day when he was to be shot, Mr. Coffin called on a Presbyterian pastor, Rev. Mr. Smith, and found that he had retired to his bed, sick on account of the approaching doom for one whom he also deemed innocent. He rose, and, proceeding to the parlor, told "Carleton" that he heard the President had "made up his mind" to have the young man executed, and forbade all admittance to those who would plead for him: so the clergyman had been asking for deliverance of One whose ear is ever open. The two proceeded to the White House, were denied admittance to the President, but wrote a note to him, begging the young man's life, which the President consented to receive; and they left the White House ignorant of the result. The next day the pardon was

* Rev. Newman Hall, London.

announced; and two hearts at least were happy at the news, though they could not know how far they had been instrumental in securing the pardon. One thing they knew, — that the President was as glad to pardon as they to hear of it.

The following is from a newspaper * correspondent, and shows the President's appreciation of their efforts who fought bravely for their country: —

"That night I left the fortress, and got Worden safe home in Washington City; when, leaving him to the care of my wife, I went with the Secretary to the President, and gave him the particulars of the engagement. As soon as I had done, Mr. Lincoln said, 'Gentlemen, I am going to shake hands with that man;' and presently he walked round with me to our little house. I led him up stairs to the room where Worden was lying with fresh bandages over his scorched eyes and face, and said, 'Jack, here's the President, who has come to see you.' He raised himself on his elbow as Mr. Lincoln took him by the hand, and said, 'You do me great honor, Mr. President; and I am only sorry that I can't see you.' The President was visibly affected, as, with tall frame and earnest gaze, he bent over his wounded subordinate; but, after a pause, he said, with a quiver in the tone of his voice, 'You have done *me* more honor, sir, than I can ever do to you.' He then sat down, while Worden gave him an account of the battle; and, on leaving, he promised, if he could legally do so, that he would make him a captain."

President Lincoln was accustomed to visit the hospitals, and speak kind words to the sick and wounded soldiers. True charity is shown not only in almsgiving, but in kind words and pleasant smiles; and many a poor

* "Advertiser."

soldier-boy, far away from home and dear ones whom he longs to see, has been cheered by beholding the President's tall form enter the crowded hospital, and, with a manner showing his fatherly interest, pass around among his "boys," as he called them. They called him "Uncle

THE PRESIDENT'S VISIT TO A HOSPITAL.

Abe;" and one such visit from him, in whose countenance they could read the real interest he felt for them, was enough to bind their loyal hearts still more firmly to him, and to the cause which he represented. More than one bereaved family to-day blesses the memory of Abraham Lincoln as they remember how he cheered in his hour of sickness, and even, it might be, beneath the shadowing wing of the death-angel, the dear soldier-boy whom they gave to their country.

President Lincoln declares plainly, and in so doing manifests his own faith in God, that a power beyond himself led to many of the wisest acts of his administration. In the letter to A. G. Hodges, where he speaks of his course in regard to slavery, saying, "When, early in the war, Gen. Frémont attempted military emancipation, I forbade it, because I did not then think it an indispensable necessity; when, a little later, Gen. Cameron, then Secretary of War, suggested the arming of the blacks, I then objected, because I did not yet think it an indispensable necessity; when, still later, Gen. Hunter attempted military emancipation, I again forbade it, because I did not yet think the indispensable necessity had come," &c, — he concludes with these words, concerning the most Christian deed of his whole life: —

"I claim not to have controlled events, but confess plainly that events have controlled me. Now, at the end of three years' struggle, the nation's condition is not what either party or any man desired or expected. God alone can claim it. Whither it is tending seems plain. If God now wills the removal of a great wrong, and wills also that we of the North, as well as you of the South, shall pay fairly for our complicity in that wrong, impartial history will find therein new cause to attest and review the justice and goodness of God."

No place may be more fitting, perhaps, than this chapter, for those words spoken at Gettysburg, Nov. 19, 1863, which indicate so plainly his deep appreciation of that patriotism which was willing to die for country and God, and which reveal the tenderness of his spirit. They are as follows: —

"Fourscore and seven years ago, our fathers brought forth upon this continent a new nation, conceived in liberty, and dedicated to the proposition, that all men are created equal. Now we are engaged in a great civil war, testing whether that nation, or any nation so conceived and so dedicated, can long endure. We are met on a great battle-field of that war. We are met to dedicate a portion of it as the final resting-place of those who here gave their lives that a nation might live. It is altogether fitting and proper that we should do this.

"But, in a larger sense, we cannot dedicate, we cannot consecrate, we cannot hallow, this ground. The brave men, living or dead, who struggled here, have consecrated it far above any power to add or detract. The world will little note, nor long remember, what we say here; but it can never forget what they did here. It is for us, the living, rather, to be dedicated here to the unfinished work that they have thus far so nobly carried on. It is rather for us to be here dedicated to the great task remaining before us, — that from these honored dead we take increased devotion to the cause for which they here highly resolved that the dead shall not have died in vain; that the nation shall, under God, have a new birth of freedom; and that the government of the people, by the people, and for the people, shall not perish from the earth."

It is well known that the President was fond of a poem entitled —

"Oh! why should the spirit of mortal be proud?"

It is a poem, a love for which indicates a spirit of true humility on the part of one who prefers it. Mr. Carpenter says, "The circumstances under which this copy was written are these: I was with the President alone one evening in his room, during the time I was painting my large picture at the White House last year. He presently threw aside his pen and papers, and began to talk to me of Shakspeare. He sent little 'Tad,' his son, into the library to bring a copy of the plays, and then read to me several of his favorite passages, showing genuine appreciation of the great poet. Relapsing into a sadder strain, he laid his book aside, and, leaning back in his chair, said, 'There's a poem which has been a great favorite with me for years, which was first shown to me, when a young man, by a friend, and which I afterwards saw, and cut from a newspaper, and learned by heart. I would,' he continued, 'give a great deal to know who wrote it; but I have never been able to ascertain.'"

Then, half closing his eyes, he repeated to me the lines which I enclose to you. Greatly pleased and interested, I told him I would like, if ever an opportunity occurred, to write them down. He said he would some time try to give them to me. A few days afterward, he asked me to accompany him to the temporary studio of Mr. Swayne, the sculptor, who was making a bust of him at the Treasury Department. While he was sitting for the bust, I was suddenly reminded of the poem, and said to him that THEN would be a good time to dictate to me. He complied; and sitting upon some books at his feet, as nearly as I can remember, I wrote the lines down, one by one, as they fell from his lips."

The first stanza reads thus: —

"Oh! why should the spirit of mortal be proud?
Like a fast-flitting meteor, a fast-flying cloud,
A flash of the lightning, a break of the wave,
He passes from life to his rest in the grave."

The closing stanza is as follows: —

"'Tis the twink of an eye, 'tis the draught of a breath,
From the blossom of health to the paleness of death,
From the gilded saloon to the bier and the shroud:
Oh! why should the spirit of mortal be proud?"

There may well be added to this chapter the following letter written by the President to Mrs. Eliza P. Gurney, an American lady, the widow of the late well-known

Friend and philanthropist, Joseph John Gurney, one of the wealthiest bankers of London: —

"My esteemed Friend, — I have not forgotten, probably never shall forget, the very impressive occasion when yourself and friends visited me on a sabbath forenoon two years ago. Nor had your kind letter, written nearly a year later, ever been forgotten. In all it has been your purpose to strengthen my reliance in God. I am much indebted to the good Christian people of the country for their constant prayers and consolations, and to no one of them more than to yourself. The purposes of the Almighty are perfect and must prevail, though we erring mortals may fail accurately to perceive them in advance. We hoped for a happy termination of this terrible war long before this; but God knows best, and has ruled otherwise. We shall yet acknowledge his wisdom and our own errors therein: meanwhile, we must work earnestly in the best lights he gives us, trusting that so working still conduces to the great end he ordains. Surely he intends some great good to follow this mighty commotion, which no mortal could make, and no mortal could stay.

"Your people, the Friends, have had, and are having, very great trials, on principles and faith opposed to both war and oppression. They can only practically oppose oppression by war. In this hard dilemma, some have chosen one horn, and some the other.

"For those appealing to me on conscientious grounds, I have done, and shall do, the best I could and can, in my own conscience, under my oath to the law. That you believe this, I doubt not; and, believing it, I shall still receive for our country and myself your earnest prayers to our Father in heaven.

"Your sincere friend,

"A. Lincoln."

In closing this record of the Christian words and deeds of our late President, it may be well to add that many more incidents might be given, did the limits of this volume allow. Enough has been given to show, that, whatever his peculiar belief on religious topics of a doctrinal character, at heart and in his life he was a child of God, and "*lived religion.*"

> "For modes of faith, let graceless zealots fight:
> His can't be wrong whose life is in the right." *

President Lincoln's life was right. He was ever giving the cup of cold water; and, verily, he shall receive a righteous man's reward.

* Pope's "Essay on Man."

CHAPTER XI.

CHOSEN AGAIN.

"Not lightly fall beyond recall
The written scrolls a breath can float:
The crowning fact, the kingliest act
Of freedom, is the freeman's vote.

. . . .

So shall our voice of sovereign choice
Swell the deep bass of duty done,
And strike the key of time to be,
When God and man shall speak as one."

WHITTIER.

"But the Lord said unto him, Go thy way, for he is a chosen vessel unto me; . . . for I will show him how great things he must suffer for my name's sake." — ACTS ix. 15, 16.

IN the sixth chapter, the course pursued by the President during the troublous times in which he governed was traced up to a certain point; though, designedly, not as minutely as a history of those times would require. The succeeding chapters have had reference more particularly to the *man* whom God gave to those times. Reference will now be had, briefly, to the course of events. These were of various character; sometimes bright with victory, sometimes shadowed with defeat.

"The ten months which divide the fall of Fort Donelson (Feb. 16, 1862) from the battle of Fredericksburg (Dec. 13, 1862) constitute the depressing era of military uncertainty. Administrative ability, executive resolution and hardihood, were never more impressively displayed than during this disheartening period; but, in spite of it, inconstant victory seemed to vibrate between the hostile banners.

"The encouraging results of Iuka and Corinth, and the opening of the Upper Mississippi, inspired the national heart with new confidence in the protection of Heaven and in the heroism of our Western soldiers. Brave old Farragut earns the grade of Admiral, and the sobriquet Salamander, by leading his thundering armada through the *feu d'enfer* which belched from Fort Philip on the right, and Fort Jackson on the left; and the martial and financial heart of the Rebellion in the South-west is palsied when the guns of his fleet sweep the streets of New Orleans, and the Tamer of Cities hangs up its scalp in his wigwam. War surges and resurges over the devoted plains of Missouri and Arkansas. The Peninsular campaign, with its checkered fortunes, alternately excites exultation and wailing; but its final failure plants in the national heart the seeds of despair, while the whirlwind which devours the army of Pope constrains us to doubt the justice of God. The victories of South Mountain and Antietam, fairly costing their weight in gore, and turning to ashes in our grasp, failed to re-animate our hopes; while Pittsburg Landing and Shiloh are more than counterpoised by the heart-rending butchery of Fredericksburg. . . . The definitive proclamation was promulged on the first of January, 1863; and it seems instantly to have been visited with that 'gracious favor' which it so reverently implores. From that eventful date, Federal ascendency flows surely and steadily on to the capture of Richmond and the surrender of Lee. Reverses and checks, it is true, intervene; but they are only eddies in the Amazon. During these twenty-seven controlling months of the war, into which more general engagements were crowded than into any equal period of the world's history, the loss of but one attests the advent of higher inspiration and divine re-enforcement to our struggling cause. The ink with which the proclamation is written is scarcely dry upon the parchment before the decisive victory of Murfreesborough expels invasion from Southern Tennessee. On the nation's birthday which next follows it, propitious Heaven almost visibly interfered by breaking the last barrier which prevents the 'loyal Father of Waters' from flowing free and unobstructed through the divided Rebellion, and by sweeping back from the bristling hills of Gettysburg the army of the alien in its last desperate raid into the bosom of the North. Away up in mid air, on the cloud-capped crests of the South-eastern Alleghanies, there is the roar and lurid flame of battle, as if the pent-up fires of the caverns of earth were bursting from their thunder-riven summits; while down, down in the deep valley, it seems as if the elements of Nature were battering chasms and pathways through their granite foundations. The gates of Georgia yield to the flushed battalions of the Cumberland; and, from the Altamaha to Cape Fear, three great States of the Confederacy soon

> "Feel the rider's tread,
> And know the conquered knee."

Hood is hurled by his infatuated chieftain against the battlements of Nashville, only to be dashed back broken and destroyed. The vale of the Shenandoah is swept by the besom and scourged by the wrath of Sheridan. Over the forest which sweeps from the Rapidan to the James, there hangs, in early spring-time, a dark and portentous cloud: the Wilderness is red, as if untimely autumn had purpled its foliage. We dimly hear, far in its resounding depths, that awe-inspiring roll, that sharp, suggestive rattle, which forewarns and terrifies nations; and ever and anon a woe-begone messenger, such as

> 'Drew Priam's curtain at the dead of night,
> And told him half his Troy was buried,'

breaks from the sequestered thicket, with a tantalizing tale of the fierce, sanguinary, but indecisive shock and recoil of embattled hosts. What weeks of heart-rending surprise! But finally, from the saturnalia of death and butchery, long rampant in its sombre and haunted recesses, he of the iron will and inflexible tenacity at length emerges in the resplendent robes of victory, and day after day for persistent months, unmoved by clamor, undismayed by failure, unwearied by resistance, slowly tightens an irresistible coil round the wailing capital of sin, until, faint and gasping, it falls into the arms of a negro brigade. City after city, harbor after harbor, succumb. The coast is hermetically sealed from Norfolk to Galveston, and the magazines and arsenals of England and France no longer pour their strengthening tides into the decaying veins of the worn-out Confederacy. Sheridan rolls up the Confederate right like a scroll, and hangs on its flying flank with the scent of a hound and the snap of a terrier. Lee surrenders his decimated horde; and over the old, endeared, precious inheritance, from the Rappahanock to the Sabine, up flies the banner, down droops the rag." *

A more eloquent description of the events which transpired from the dawn of freedom for an enfranchised race, to the dawn of peace for a redeemed nation, could scarcely be penned. And, all the while that these events were transpiring, President Lincoln was sending up from the White House his fervent prayers, and forth to our

* Hon. H. C. Deming.

brave soldiers his earnest sympathy. All the while the Government was upheld, and unfaltering hearts kept close to the national flag, though it was torn and gory.

"Is there an element of stress and pressure that could be brought to bear on any Government that was not brought to bear upon ours? Confessedly there was a stress upon it which no other Government could have borne. Upon a people, all whose habits and interests and tastes were those of peace, there was suddenly sprung a war, and not merely that, but a civil war, and one unprecedented in its gigantic proportions. Then at a moment, and under circumstances of the greatest disadvantage, came the call for men; and they went. It came for more and more,—'six hundred thousand more;' and the men were ready. Next, and to a people always charged with loving money over-much, came the call for money; and the money was ready. Taxes came in new forms; but not only were they paid, the people were clamorous for them. Money was poured out like water, and as never before, for bounties, as a loan to the Government, for the Sanitary and Christian Commissions, for the refugees and freedmen. Meantime battles were disastrous; faint-heartedness, and even treason, were not wanting in the North; our English friends pronounced our cause hopeless, and did what they could to make it so; homes were desolated; the wounded and maimed walked our streets, and the sickening wail of exposure and starvation came up from Southern prisons. In the midst of all this came a new and unheard-of trial,—the popular election of a Chief Magistrate by a great nation in time of civil war. How solemn, how grand, how quiet, how decisive, was that day! It was the noblest triumph of the war, — its turning-point, — the turning-point in the destiny of our country." *

The presidential election took place on the 8th of November, 1864, and resulted in the triumph of Mr. Lincoln in every loyal State except Kentucky, New Jersey, and Delaware. In some of the States, their soldiers in the field were allowed to vote; and the military vote was almost invariably cast for Lincoln and Johnson. The official returns for the entire vote polled summed up 4,034,789. Of these, Mr. Lincoln received 2,223,035, and McClellan received 1,811,754; leaving a majority of 411,281 on the popular vote. Mr. Lincoln was elected by a plurality in 1860. In 1864, his majority was decided and unmistakable.

At a late hour on the night of the election, the President was serenaded by a club of Pennsylvanians, and he thus responded: —

"FRIENDS AND FELLOW-CITIZENS, — Even before I had been informed by you that this compliment was paid me by loyal citizens of Pennsylvania friendly to me, I had inferred that you were of that portion of my countrymen who think that the best interests of the nation are to be subserved by the support of the present Administration. I do not pretend to say that you who think so embrace all the patriotism and loyalty of the country; but I do believe, and, I trust, without personal interest, that the welfare of the country does require that such support and indorsement be given. I earnestly believe that the consequences of this day's work, if it be as you assume, and as now seems probable, will be to the lasting advantage, if not to the very salvation, of the country. I can-

* Rev. Mark Hopkins, D.D.

not at this hour say what has been the result of the election; but, whatever it may be, I have no desire to modify this opinion,—that all who have labored to-day in behalf of the Union organization have wrought for the best interest of their country and the world, not only for the present, but for all future ages. I am thankful to God for this approval of the people; but, while deeply grateful for this mark of their confidence in me, if I know my heart, my gratitude is free from any taint of personal triumph. I do not impugn the motives of any one opposed to me. It is no pleasure to me to triumph over any one; but I give thanks to the Almighty for this evidence of the people's resolution to stand by free government and the rights of humanity."

On the 6th of December, 1864, the President sent to Congress his usual annual message. How little any one dreamed that it was his last! It spoke of unchanged views in regard to the slave, and expressed a desire for peace in these decisive words: "In stating a single condition of peace, I mean simply to say that the war will cease on the part of the Government whenever it shall have ceased on the part of those who began it."

On his way to Washington to fill the chair of the President, Mr. Lincoln spoke at Steubenville of the fact, that, if a President should adopt a wrong policy, the opportunity to condemn him would occur in four years' time: "Then," he added, "I can be turned out, and a better man, with better views, be put in my place." But *the people* were satisfied. They, the majority, knew of no better man; and so he whom God had appointed took the chair a second time. The following is his second inaugural address:—

"FELLOW-CITIZENS,—At this second appearing to take the oath of the presidential office, there is less occasion for an extended address than there was at first. Then a statement somewhat in detail of a course to be pursued seemed very fitting and proper. Now, at the expiration of four years, during which public declarations have been constantly called forth on every point and place of the great contest which still absorbs the attention, and engrosses the energies, of the nation, little that is new could be presented.

"The progress of our arms — upon which all else chiefly depends — is as well known to the public as to myself; and it is, I trust, reasonably satisfactory and encouraging to all. With high hopes for the future, no prediction in regard to it is ventured.

"On the occasion corresponding to this four years ago, all thoughts were anxiously directed to an impending civil war. All dreaded it; all sought to avoid it. While the inaugural address was being delivered from this place, devoted altogether to saving the Union without war, insurgent agents were in the city seeking to destroy it without war, seeking to dissolve the Union, and divide the effects by negotiation.

"Both parties deprecated war; but one of them would make war rather than let the nation survive, and the other would accept war rather than let it perish; and the war came.

"One-eighth of the whole population were colored slaves, not distributed generally over the Union, but located in the Southern part of it. These slaves constituted a peculiar and powerful interest. All knew that this interest was somehow the cause of the war. To strengthen, perpetuate, and extend this interest was the object for which the insurgents would rend the Union by war, while the Government claimed no right to do more than to restrict the territorial enlargement of it.

"Neither party expected for the war the magnitude or the duration which it has already attained. Neither anticipated that the cause of the conflict might cease, even before the conflict itself should cease. Each looked for an easier triumph, and a result less fundamental and astounding.

"Both read the same Bible, and pray to the same God, and each invokes his aid against the other. It may seem strange that any men should dare to ask a just God's assistance in wringing their bread from the sweat of other men's faces; but let us judge not, that we be not judged. The prayers of both should not be answered. That of neither has been answered fully. The Almighty has his own purposes. Woe unto the world because of offences! for it must needs be that offences come; but woe to that man by whom the offence cometh! If we shall suppose that American slavery is one of these offences, which in the providence of God must needs come, but which, having continued through his appointed time, he now wills to remove, and that he gives to both North and South this terrible war as the woe due to those by whom the offence came, shall we discern there is any departure from those divine attributes which the believers in a living God always ascribe to him? Fondly do we hope, fervently do we pray, that this mighty scourge of war may speedily pass away. Yet if God wills that it continue until all the wealth piled by the bondman's two hundred and fifty years of unrequited toil shall be sunk, and until every drop of blood drawn with the lash shall be paid by another drawn by the sword, as was said three thousand years ago, so still it must be said, the judgments of the Lord are true and righteous altogether.

"With malice towards none, with charity for all, with

firmness in the right as God gives us to see the right, let us strive on to finish the work we are in; to bind up the nation's wound; to care for him who shall have borne the battle, and for his widow and orphans; to do all which may achieve and cherish a just and lasting peace among ourselves and with all nations."

We see the spirit which breathes in this inaugural, and we cannot but love the memory of the man who wrote it.

"The most unsparing criticism, denunciation, and ridicule never moved him to a single bitter expression, never seemed to awaken in him a single bitter thought. The most exultant hour of party victory brought no exultation to him. He accepted power, not as an honor, but as a responsibility; and when, after a severe struggle, that power came a second time into his hands, there was something preternatural in the calmness of his acceptance of it. The first impulse seemed to be a disclaimer of all triumph over the party that had strained their utmost to push him from his seat, and then a sober girding-up of his loins to go on with the work to which he was appointed.

"The last inaugural was characterized by a tone so peculiarly solemn, and free from earthly passion, that it seems to us now, who look back on it in the light of what followed, as if his soul had already parted from earthly things, and felt the powers of the world to come. It was not the formal State-paper of the chief of a party in an hour of victory, so much as the solemn soliloquy of a great soul reviewing its course under a vast responsibility, and appealing from all earthly judgments to the tribunal of Infinite Justice. It was the solemn clearing of his soul for the great sacrament of death; and the words that he quoted in it with such thrilling power were those of the adoring spirits that veil their faces before the throne: 'Just and true are thy ways, thou King of saints.'"*

The course pursued by the President is indorsed by the people in the act of continuing him in the office which he had so faithfully filled. This was the laurel wreath with which they crowned him as a conqueror, little dreaming that the angels were already preparing a garland of immortelles for the brow of the people's President, whose brightness and beauty would remain undimmed forever.

* Mrs. Stowe, in "Atlantic Monthly," August, 1865.

CHAPTER XII.

LAST DAYS AND A NATION'S GRIEF.

"This Duncan
Hath borne his faculties so meek, hath been
So clear in his great office, that his virtues
Will plead like angels, trumpet-tongued, against
The deep damnation of his taking-off."
SHAKSPEARE'S *Macbeth.*

"Man goeth to his long home, and the mourners go about the streets." —
ECCLES. xii. 5.

THE hour of triumph arrives. Victory no longer hovers between the contending forces, but settles down upon the standard of freedom. Grant and Sherman and Sheridan have done their work bravely; and they and their fellow-warriors, officers and privates, have won immortal honor; for "Richmond is ours!" Lee retreats! Grant pursues! The Confederate President is a flying fugitive; and he whom God called to be the savior of a race is to tread the streets of the conquered city, — the Babylon that had fallen!

"Carleton" * narrates in his own graphic style the visit of the President to Richmond, calling it "one of the memorable events of the week." He says, "There was no committee of reception, no guard of honor, no grand display of troops, no assembling of an eager multitude to welcome him. He entered the city unheralded. Six sailors, armed with carabines, stepped upon the shore, followed by the President, who held his little son by the hand; and Admiral Porter: the officers followed, and six more sailors brought up the rear."

* C. C. Coffin, Esq., in "Atlantic Monthly" for June, 1865.

Mr. Coffin himself was there, and speaks throughout as an eye-witness: —

"There were forty or fifty freedmen, who had been sole possessors of themselves for twenty-four hours, at work on the bank of the canal, securing some floating timber, under the direction of a lieutenant. Somehow they obtained the information that the man who was head and shoulders taller than all others around him, with features large and irregular, with a mild eye and pleasant countenance, was President Lincoln.

"'God bless you, sah!' said one, taking off his cap, and bowing very low.

"'Hurrah, hurrah! President Linkum hab come!' was the shout which rang through the street.

"The lieutenant found himself without a command. What cared those freedmen, fresh from the house of bondage, for floating timber and military commands? Their deliverer had come, — he who, next to the Lord Jesus, was their best friend. It was not an hurrah that they gave, but a wild, jubilant cry of inexpressible joy.

"They gathered round the President, ran ahead, hovered upon the flanks of the little company, and hung like a dark cloud upon the rear. Men, women, and children joined the constantly-increasing throng. They came from all the by-streets, running in breathless haste, shouting, hallooing, and dancing with delight. The men threw up their hats; the women waved their bonnets and handkerchiefs, clapped their hands, and sang, 'Glory to God! glory, glory, glory!' rendering all the praise to God, who had heard their wailings in the past, their moanings for wives, husbands, children, and friends sold out of their sight, had given them freedom, and, after long years of waiting, had permitted them thus unexpectedly to behold the face of their great benefactor.

"'I thank you, dear Jesus, that I behold President Linkum!' was the exclamation of a woman who stood upon the threshold of her humble home, and, with streaming eyes and clasped hands, gave thanks aloud to the savior of men.

"Another, more demonstrative in her joy, was jumping, and striking her hands with all her might, crying, 'Bless de Lord, bless de Lord, bless de Lord!' as if there could be no end of her thanksgiving.

"The air rang with a tumultuous chorus of voices. The streets became almost impassable on account of the increasing multitude. Soldiers were summoned to clear the way. How strange the event! The President of the United States — he who had been hated, despised, maligned, above all other men living; to whom the vilest epithets had been applied by the people of Richmond — was walking their streets, receiving thanksgiving, blessings, and prayers from thousands who hailed him as an ally of the Messiah! . . .

"Abraham Lincoln was walking their streets; and, worst of all, that plain, honest-hearted man was recognizing the 'niggers' as human beings by returning their salutations! The walk was long, and the President halted a moment to rest. 'May de good Lord bless you, President Linkum!' said an old negro, removing his hat, and bowing, with tears of joy rolling down his cheeks. The President removed his own hat, and bowed in silence; but it was a bow which upset the forms, laws, customs, and ceremonies of centuries. It was a death-shock to chivalry, and a mortal wound to caste. Recognize a nigger! Faugh! A woman in an adjoining house beheld it, and turned from the scene in unspeakable disgust. There were men in the crowd who had daggers in their eyes; but the chosen assassin was not there, the hour for the damning work had not come, and that great-hearted man passed on to the Executive Mansion of the Confederacy.

"Want of space compels us to pass over other scenes, —the visit of the President to the State House; the jubilant shouts of the crowd; the rush of freedmen into the Capitol grounds, where, till the appearance of their deliverer, they had never been permitted to enter; the ride of the President through the streets; his visit to Libby Prison; the distribution of bread to the destitute," &c.

While reminded of Washington returning the salute of a negro because he would not be outdone in politeness, none can fail to recognize even more than politeness in Lincoln's act of courtesy. It was justice, strict, impartial justice, that lowered the brow of the conqueror to the salutation of the delivered.

Joy filled the North. Bells were rung with jubilant and untiring energy. Cannons bayed the nation's joy. Everywhere there was gladness on human faces. Men clasped hands joyously, and the words "victory" and "peace" were on every tongue. Even those whose dear ones would never return from the field of battle thanked God, with tearful eyes and aching hearts, that such precious blood had not been shed in vain. Drafting and recruiting was stopped in the loyal States, and "all went merry as a marriage-bell." Scarcely had the people ceased shouting over the fall of Richmond, when there came tidings of the surrender of Lee; and again the bells and cannon were heard, and glad hearts thanked God for the news.

But, hark! the jubilant bells cease. On the air at midnight, in more than one city in our land, comes the solemn stroke of the death-knell. What can it portend? Roused from slumber by the unwelcome sound, the people learn the sad and shocking tidings that their beloved President had been stricken down by an assassin's hand, and lay bleeding and dying in the capital of the nation.

The morning papers tell in staring capitals the horrid tale: "The President is insensible, life is slowly ebbing away," is the telegraphic message from one who watched at his side; and before nine A.M., on the 15th of April, 1865, flags hang at half-mast, minute-guns are sounding, bells toll, tears fill the eyes of strong men, and women and children weep, as for their own beloved dead; for President Lincoln is with us no longer. Slavery struck its final blow, and orphaned the nation.

Wearied with the incessant cares of his office, the President sometimes sought rest and relaxation from stern duties by attending the theatre, listening to the elocutional powers of the performers, and beholding the success with which the actors "held the mirror up to nature."

On the night of the 14th of April, 1865, he attended Ford's Theatre in Washington, partly for a respite and rest, and partly that the people, who expected his presence, might not be disappointed. He did not dream of immediate danger. Many at the North were uneasy at the fact that the President was exposed to danger in Richmond; but he did not fear. To a friend who expressed the idea that the rebels might attempt his life, he said, stepping to a desk, and drawing from a pigeon-hole a package of letters, "There, every one of these contains a threat to assassinate me. I might be nervous if I were to dwell upon the subject; but I have come to the conclusion that there are opportunities to kill me every day of my life, if there are persons disposed to do it. It is not possible to avoid exposure to such a fate, and I shall not trouble myself about it."

So he attended the theatre, without taking precautions against the assassin who came, all unannounced, to his unguarded victim. "The play was 'Our American Cousin.' While all were intent upon its representation, the report of a pistol first announced the presence of the assassin,* who uttered the word "Freedom!" and advanced toward the front. Major Rathbone having discerned the murderer through the smoke, and grappled with him, the latter dropped his pistol, and aimed with a knife at the breast of his antagonist, who caught the blow on the upper part of his left arm, but was unable to detain the desperado, though he immediately seized him again. The villain, however, leaped some twelve feet down upon the open stage, tangling his spur in the draped flag below the box, and stumbling in his fall.

"Recovering himself immediately, he flourished his dagger, shouted '*Sic semper tyrannis!*' and 'The South is avenged!' then retreated successfully through the labyrinth of the theatre — perfectly familiar to him — to his horse in waiting below. Between the deed of blood and the escape, there was not the lapse of a minute. The hour was about half-past ten. There was but one pursuer, and he from the audience; but he was outstripped.

"The meaning of the pistol-shot was soon ascertained. Mr. Lincoln had been shot in the back of the head, behind the left ear, the ball traversing an oblique line to the right ear. He was rendered instantly unconscious, and never knew friends or pain again. Having been conveyed as soon as possible to a house opposite the theatre, he expired there the next morning at twenty-two minutes past seven o'clock, attended by the principal members

* J. Wilkes Booth.

of his cabinet, and other friends; from all of whom the heart-rending spectacle drew copious tears of sorrow. Mrs. Lincoln and her son Robert were in an adjoining apartment; the former bowed down with anguish, the

THE DEATH OF MR. LINCOLN.

latter strong enough to sustain and console her. Soon after nine o'clock, the body was removed to the White House under military escort."

There the body was embalmed, and prepared for the grave. The paraphernalia of mourning, in this case no heartless display, filled the house. In the east room, the solemn funeral services were first performed. "Near the centre of the room stood the grand catafalque, upon which rested the mortal remains of the illustrious dead, enclosed in a beautiful mahogany coffin lined with lead, and with a white satin covering over the metal. It was finished in the most elaborate style, with four silver handles on each side, stars glistening between the handles, and a vein of silver winding around the whole case in a serpentine form. To the edges of the lid hung a nice silver tassel, making a chaste and elaborate fringe to the whole case. The silver plate bore the simple inscription: —

ABRAHAM LINCOLN,

SIXTEENTH PRESIDENT OF THE UNITED STATES.

Born February 12, 1809;

Died April 15, 1865.

"The catafalque stood lengthwise to the room, or north and south, and immediately in front of the double doors which lead to the side hall. The floor of the catafalque was about four feet in height, and approached by one step on all sides, making it easy to view the face of the honored dead. Above this was a canopy, in an arched form, lined on the under-side with white fluted satin, covered otherwise with black velvet and crape. This was supported by four posts, heavily incased with the emblem of mourning. The canopy, the posts, and the main body of the catafalque, were festooned with crape, and fastened at each fold with rosettes of black satin.

"On the top of the coffin lay three wreaths of moss and evergreen, with white plumes and lilies intermingled. At the head of the coffin, standing upon the floor of the catafalque, and leaning against the metallic case, stood a beautiful cross, made of japonicas, lilies, and other white flowers, as bright and blooming as though they were still on their parent-stem, and had not been plucked to adorn the house of the dead; its pure and immaculate white furnishing a strong contrast with the deep black on all sides. On the foot of the coffin lay an anchor of flowers. Encircling the coffin, in a serpentine form, was a vine of evergreens studded with pure white flowers; and within its meandering folds were deposited several wreaths of the same material. These had all been brought by some friendly hands, the tokens of love and affection, and deposited around and near the case that contained the mortal remains of the man who had been near and dear to them. Here, then, were the emblems of the dead, the marks of rank, the tokens of grief, deep and sorrowful, and happiness hereafter, as well as hope and immortality in the future. Surely the scene in honor to the illustrious dead was a worthy exhibition of the love, esteem, and pride of a free people in their fallen chief,—fallen, too, in the midst of his usefulness, and just when his greatness and goodness were being recognized by all." *

A newspaper, speaking of those present at his funeral-service, says, "Close by the corpse sat the relatives of the deceased,—plain, honest, hardy people, typical as much of the simplicity of our institutions as of Mr. Lincoln's self-made eminence. No blood-relatives of Mr. Lincoln were to be found. It is a singular evidence of the poverty of his origin, and therefore of his exceeding good report, that, excepting his immediate family, none answering to his name could be discovered. Mrs. Lincoln's relations were present, however, in some force: Dr. Lyman Beecher Todd, Gen. John B. S. Todd, C. M. Smith, Esq., and Mr. N. W. Edwards, the late President's brother-in-law. Plain, self-made people were here, and were sincerely affected. Capt. Robert Lincoln sat during the services with his face in his handkerchief, weeping quietly; and little Tad, his face red and heated, cried as if his heart would break. Mrs. Lincoln, weak now, and nervous, did not enter the east room, nor follow the remains. She was the Chief Magistrate's lady yesterday; to-day, a widow bearing only an immortal name."

* "Lincoln Memorial."

Clergymen of different religious denominations, as was eminently fitting, took part in the funeral exercises. Rev. Dr. Hall, of the Episcopal Church in Washington, opened the services by reading the beautiful service of his church for the burial of the dead. Bishop Simpson, of the Methodist-Episcopal Church of Illinois, then offered prayer. The funeral oration was next delivered by Rev. P. D. Gurley, D.D., a Presbyterian pastor, of Washington, in whose church the President and family were accustomed to worship. The services closed with a prayer by Dr. Gray, chaplain of the United-States Senate. In his oration, whose text was, "Have faith in God" (Mark xi. 22), Dr. Gurley said,—

"As we stand here to-day, mourners around this coffin and around the lifeless remains of our beloved Chief Magistrate, we recognize and we adore the sovereignty of God. . . . It was a cruel, cruel hand, that dark hand of the assassin, which smote our honored, wise, and noble President, and filled the land with sorrow. But above and beyond that hand there is another which we must see and acknowledge,—it is the chastening hand of a wise and a faithful Father."

After continuing for some time in this strain, endeavoring to comfort the mourners gathered there, he spoke of the departed thus: "The people confided in the late lamented President with a full and loving confidence. Probably no man since the days of Washington was ever so deeply and firmly embedded and enshrined in the very hearts of the people as Abraham Lincoln. Nor was it a mistaken confidence and love. He deserved it, deserved it well, deserved it all. He merited it by his character, by his acts, and by the whole tenor and tone and spirit of his life. He was simple and sincere, plain and honest, truthful and just, benevolent and kind. His perceptions were quick and clear, his judgments were calm and accurate, and his purposes were good and pure beyond question. Always and everywhere he aimed and endeavored to *be* right and to *do* right. His integrity was thorough, all-pervading, all-controlling, and incorruptible. It was the same in every place and relation, in the consideration and the control of matters great or small, — the same firm and steady principle of power and beauty, that shed a clear and crowning lustre upon all his other excellences of mind and heart, and recommended him to his fellow-citizens as *the* man, who in a time of unexampled peril, when the very life of the nation was at stake, should be chosen to occupy in the country, and for the country, its highest post of power and responsibility. How wisely and well, how purely and faithfully, how firmly and steadily, how justly and successfully, he did occupy that post, and meet its grave demands, in circumstances of surpassing trial and difficulty, is known to you all, known to the country and to the world. He comprehended from the first the perils to which treason had exposed the freest and best government on the earth, the vasts interests of liberty and humanity that were to be saved or lost forever in the urgent impending conflict: he rose to the dignity and momentousness of the occasion; saw his duty as the Chief Magistrate of a great and imperilled people; and he determined to *do* his duty, and his whole duty, seeking the guidance and leaning on the arm of Him of whom it is written, 'He giveth power to the faint; and to them that have no might he increaseth strength.' Yes: he leaned upon *his* arm. He recognized and received the truth, 'that the kingdom is the Lord's, and he is the Governor among the nations.' He remembered that 'God is in history,' and he felt that nowhere had

18

his hand and his mercy been so marvellously conspicuous as in the history of this nation. He hoped and he prayed that that same hand would continue to guide us, and that same mercy continue to abound to us in the time of our greatest need. I speak what I know, and testify what I have often heard him say, when I affirm that that guidance and mercy were the props on which he humbly and habitually leaned: they were the best hope he had for himself and for his country. Hence, when he was leaving his home in Illinois, and coming to this city to take his seat in the Executive Chair of a disturbed and troubled nation, he said to the old and tried friends who gathered tearfully around him, and bade him farewell, 'I leave you with this request,—*pray for me.*' They did pray for him, and millions of others prayed for him; nor did they pray in vain. Their prayer was heard, and the answer appears in all his subsequent history: it shines forth with a heavenly radiance in the whole course and tenor of his administration, from its commencement to its close. God raised him up for a great and glorious mission, furnished him for his work, and aided him in its accomplishment. Nor was it merely by strength of mind, and honesty of heart, and purity and pertinacity of purpose, that he furnished him. In addition to these things, he gave him a calm and abiding confidence in the overwhelming providence of God, and in the ultimate triumph of truth and righteousness through the power and blessing of God. This confidence strengthened him in all his hours of anxiety and toil, and inspired him with calm and cheering hope when others were inclining to despondency and gloom. Never shall I forget the emphasis and the deep emotion with which he said, in this very room, to a company of clergymen and others who called to pay him their respects in the darkest days of our civil conflict, 'Gentlemen, my hope of success in this great and terrible struggle rests on that immutable foundation, the justice and goodness of God; and, when events are very threatening and prospects very dark, I still hope, that, in some way which man cannot see, all will be well in the end, because our cause is just, and God is on our side.' . . . God be praised that our fallen Chief lived long enough to see the day dawn, and the day-star of joy and peace rise upon the nation! He saw it, and was glad. Alas, alas! he only saw the *dawn*. When the *sun* has risen full-orbed and glorious, and a happy re-united people are rejoicing in its light, it will shine upon his grave; but that grave will be a precious and a consecrated spot. The friends of Liberty and of the Union will repair to it, in years and ages to come, to pronounce the memory of its occupant blessed; and gathering from his very ashes, and from the rehearsal of his deeds and virtues, fresh incentives to patriotism, they will there renew their vows of fidelity to their country and their God."

At the conclusion of the services, the body of the President was borne to the capitol. The hearse was built for the occasion, and was drawn by six gray horses.

"The funeral *cortége* started with military precision at ten o'clock. The avenue was cleared the whole length from the Presidential Mansion to the Capitol. Every window, house-top, balcony, and every inch of the sidewalks, on either side, was densely crowded with a living throng to witness the procession. In all this dense crowd, hardly a sound was heard. People conversed with each other in suppressed tones. Presently the monotonous thump of the funeral drum sounded upon the street, and the military escort of the funeral car began to march past with solemn tread, muffled drums, and arms reversed.

"A scene so solemn, imposing, and impressive as that which the national metropolis presented, and upon which myriad eyes of saddened faces were gazing, was never witnessed, under circumstances so appalling, in any portion of our beloved country. Around us is the capital city, clad in the habiliments of mourning; above us, the cloudless sky, so bright, so tranquil, so cheerful, as if heaven would, on this solemn occasion, specially invite us, by the striking contrast, to turn our thoughts from the darkness and the miseries of this life to the light and the joy that shine with endless lustre beyond it. The mournful strains of the funeral dirge, borne on the gentle zephyrs of this summer-like day, touch a responsive chord in every human heart of the countless thousands, that, with solemn demeanor and measured step, follow to their temporary resting-place, in the National Capitol, the cold, inanimate form of one, who, living, was the honored Chief Magistrate of the American people, and, dead, will ever be endeared in their fondest memories. Never did a generous and grateful people pay, in anguish and tears, a tribute more sincere or merited to a kind, humane, and patriotic chieftain; never were the dark and bloody deeds of crime brought out in relief so bold, and in horror and detestation so universal, as in the sublime and imposing honors this day tendered to the corpse of Abraham Lincoln. Such a scene is the epoch of a life-time. Strong men are deeply affected; gentle women weep; children are awe-stricken: none will ever forget it. Memory has consecrated it on her brightest tablet; and it will ever be thought, spoken, and written of, as the sublime homage of a sorrowing nation at the shrine of the martyred patriot." *

Arrived at the Capitol, Rev. Dr. Gurley offered prayer, and soon the services were over: the few who had been permitted to enter were dismissed from the rotunda, and silence reigned around the coffin of the honored dead.

"The corpse of the President was placed beneath the right concave, now streaked with the mournful trappings, and left in state, watched by guards of officers with drawn swords. This was a wonderful spectacle, — the man most beloved and honored, in the ark of the Republic. The storied paintings, representing eras in its history, were draped in sable, through which they seemed to cast reverential glances upon the lamented bier. The thrilling scenes depicted by Trumbull, the commemorative canvases of Leutze, the wilderness vegetation of Powell, glared from their separate pedestals upon the central spot where lay the fallen majesty of the country. At night the jets of gas, concealed in the spring of the dome, were lighted up, so that their bright reflection upon the frescoed walls hurled masses of burning light, like marvellous haloes, upon the little box where so much that was loved and honored rested, on its way to the grave; and so, through the starry night, in the fane of the great Union he had strengthened and recovered, the ashes of Abraham Lincoln, zealously guarded, lay in calm repose." †

The acting Secretary of State (Secretary Seward having been wounded in an attempt made to assassinate him on the same night with the President), Mr. Hunter, issued the following official document: —

* "Lincoln Memorial," p. 147. † Ibid., p. 138.

DEPARTMENT OF STATE, WASHINGTON, April 17, 1865.

TO THE PEOPLE OF THE UNITED STATES: —

The undersigned is directed to announce that the funeral ceremonies of the lamented Chief Magistrate will take place at the Executive Mansion, in this city, at twelve o'clock, noon, on Wednesday, the 19th inst. The various religious denominations throughout the country are invited to meet in their respective places of worship at that hour, for the purpose of solemnizing the occasion with appropriate ceremonies.

W. HUNTER, *Acting Secretary of State.*

Throughout the loyal States, the day of the funeral was observed, and never with more sincerity. Churches, streets, houses, stores, were draped in mourning: flags were hung at half-mast, minute-guns were fired, and congregations assembled, bowed with grief, in all the larger towns, to join in services appropriate to the day.*

* In Reading, Mass., the following hymn, written by the author of these pages, was sung by members of the Congregationalist, Universalist, and Baptist choirs, in the largest church of the town, where, as one stricken, sympathizing family, the inhabitants were gathered: —

FUNERAL HYMN. *Air,* — "*Mount Vernon.*"

Hushed to-day are sounds of gladness,
From the mountains to the sea;
And the plaintive voice of sadness
Rises, mighty God, to thee.

Freedom claimed another martyr;
Heaven received another saint:
Who are we, thy will to question?
Lord, we weep without complaint.

May we, to thy wisdom bowing,
Own thy love in this dark spell,
While with tears a mighty nation
Buries one it loved so well!

And, O Thou who took our leader,
With the Promised Land in view,
While on Pisgah's height we leave him,
Lead us, Lord, the Jordan through!

While the people sympathized with the bereaved family of the martyred President, and those who had been made widows during the war sympathized deeply with Mrs. Lincoln (to whom even the Queen of England sent an autograph letter, assuring her of the sympathy of a widowed heart), yet it was not only as those who felt for others that the people mourned. They had themselves lost a friend. They mourned with a sense of personal bereavement. Many families, whose dear ones, though exposed to the perils of the battle-field, the prison, and the hospital, had yet returned safely to their homes, now felt that they had some one for whom to weep; since President Lincoln belonged to all. Sublime utterances of faith in God, tender expressions of love for the departed, and words of solemn instruction, were heard on this day of mourning; and each loyal hand that held "the pen of a ready writer" was moved to add a tribute to the memory of the nation's martyr. Mrs. Stowe, after speaking of the rejoicings over victory, adds, —

"But this our joy has been ordained to be changed into a wail of sorrow. The kind hard hand that held the helm so steadily in the desperate tossings of the storm has been stricken down just as we entered port; the fatherly heart that bore all our sorrows can take no earthly part in our joys. His were the cares, the watchings, the toils, the agonies, of a nation in mortal struggle; and God looking down was so well pleased with his humble faithfulness, his patient continuance in well-doing, that earthly rewards and honors seemed all too poor for him; so he reached down, and took him to immortal glories. 'Well done, good and faithful servant! enter thou into the joy of thy Lord.'"*

* "Atlantic Monthly," August, 1865.

The remains of the President were borne from Washington to Springfield, where they were finally deposited, by way of Baltimore, Harrisburg, Philadelphia, New York, Albany, Buffalo, Cleveland, Columbus, and Chicago, — a distance in circuit of about eighteen hundred miles. All along the route, the people gathered with various testimonials of respect, and evidences of grief that was great and sincere.

The body rested, while in Philadelphia, in that hall, around which cluster so many historical memories, and over which, four years before, the President raised the flag of our country. "The bier was close to the famous old Liberty Bell, which first sounded forth, in 1776, the tidings of independence.

"The interior of the hall, as well as the exterior, was heavily draped and most artistically illuminated. Around the remains were appropriate decorations, leaves of exquisite evergreens, and flowers of an exquisite crimson bloom. At the head of the corpse were bouquets; beneath, the flaming tapers at the feet; from the elaborately hung walls, the portraits of the great and good dead were eloquent in their silence, and seemed to say that not one of the great actors of other eras, preserved in canvas, marble, and metal, looking down like living mourners on that honored catafalque, ever filled his space with more dignity than the dead Lincoln. Not Columbus from his brazen door; not De Soto planting his cross on the Mississippi; not Pocahontas; not Miles Standish on the "Mayflower;" not William Penn making peace with the Indians; not Benjamin Franklin in his philosophy; not the fiery Patrick Henry as he ejaculated his war-cry in the Virginia House of Delegates, nor John Adams as he shouted it in Boston; not Washington with his sword; nor Jefferson with his pen; nor Hamilton with his statesmanship; nor John Jay; nor John Marshall, the purest jurist of our earlier or later history; nor Perry, the sea-king of 1812, riding on billows of blood through a line of blazing ships; nor Jackson, with his triple triumph over savage and Briton and the spirit of incipient treason, — not one was more worthy of the genius of the poet, the painter, the sculptor, and the orator, than the gentle and illustrious patriot whose virtues and whose genius the American people now mourn." *

The limits of this volume will not permit further mention of the funeral honors. Suffice it to say that they were such as were never paid to mortal before, and showed, in some degree, the depth of the national sorrow.

Foreign nations sympathized with us in our national loss. While those who had voted against the President now mourned as sincerely as any his sad and sudden death, the event awoke sorrow in hearts abroad which had sometimes throbbed in sympathy with our enemies. England spoke through her press in terms of abhorrence that such a crime had been committed, and in words of eulogy concerning the martyred one. Earl Russell announced to the House of Lords the private letter of Queen Victoria to the President's widow. Earl Derby followed with words of sympathy.

France joined in the general horror of the crime, and sympathy with the mourners. Henri Martin, the historian, wrote an article, headed, "A great Martyr of Democracy," commencing, "Slavery, before expiring, has gathered up the remnants of its strength and rage to strike a coward blow at its conqueror." In Italy, Belgium, and Prussia, suitable notice was taken of the sorrow-

* "Lincoln Memorial," p. 176.

ful event. In Portugal, a most eloquent address was delivered in the Chamber of Peers, at Lisbon, by Sr. Rebello da Silva, from which is given the following extract: —

"Lincoln, martyr to the broad principle which he represented in power and struggle, belongs now to history and to posterity. Like Washington, whose idea he continued, his name will be inseparable from the memorable epochs to which he is bound, and which he expresses. If the defender of independence freed America, Lincoln unsheathed without hesitation the sword of the Republic, and with its point erased and tore out from the statutes of a free people the anti-social stigma, the anti-humanitarian blasphemy, the sad, shameful, infamous codicil of old societies, the dark, repugnant abuse of slavery, which Jesus Christ first condemned from the top of the cross, proclaiming the equality of man before God, which nineteen centuries of civilization, reared in the gospel, have proscribed and rejected as the opprobrium of our times."

"At the moment when he was breaking the chains of a luckless race; when he was seeing in millions of rehabilitated slaves millions of future citizens; when the bronze voice of Grant's victorious cannon was proclaiming the emancipation of the soul, of the conscience, and of toil; when the scourge was about to fall from the hands of the scourgers; when the ancient slave-pen was about to be transformed, for the captive, into a domestic altar; at the moment when the stars of the Union, sparkling and resplendent with the golden fires of Liberty, were waving over the subdued walls of Petersburg and Richmond, . . . the sepulchre opens, and the strong, the powerful, enters it. In the midst of triumphs and acclamations, there appeared to him a spectre like that of

Cæsar in the Ides of March, saying to him, 'You have lived!'

"Have lived! Yes, Lincoln did live once, in the body; and thank God, who hath made man immortal, he liveth still. He lives! He lives! He lives to-day in his imperishable example, in his recorded words of wisdom, in his great maxims of liberty and enfranchisement.

"The good never die; to them belongs endurable immortality; they perish not upon the earth, and they exist forever in heaven. The good of the present live in the future, as the good of the past are here with us and in us to-day. The great primeval lawgiver, entombed for forty centuries in that unknown grave in an obscure vale of Moab, to-day legislates in your halls of state, and preaches on all your sabbaths in your synagogues. Salem's royal singer indites our liturgies, and leads our worship. Socrates questions atheists in these streets. Phidias sculptures the friezes of Christian temples; the desecrated tongue of mangled Tully arraigns our Catilines; against the Philip of to-day the dead Demosthenes thunders; the dead Leonidas guards the gates of every empire which wrestles for its sovereignty; the dead Justinian issues in your country the living mandates of the law; the dead Martin Luther issues from your press the living oracles of God; the dead Napoleon sways France from that silent throne in the Invalides; the dead George Washington held together through wrangling decades this brotherhood of States; and the dead ABRAHAM LINCOLN will peal the clarion of beleagured nations, and marshal and beckon on the wavering battle line of liberty till the last generation of man

'Shall creation's death behold
As Adam saw her prime.'

His fame will grow brighter and grander as it descends the ages, and posterity will regard him as the incarnation of democracy in its pure childhood, as the embodiment of those ideas of universal emancipation which were the glory of its faithful epoch.

. . . "When the race shall have finally climbed to the lofty table-land of UNIVERSAL BROTHERHOOD, to which it is inevitably destined by the paramount law of its own development, and shall turn backward its wistful eye for those who have led its weary pilgrimage through passes the most perilous, and over wastes the most disheartening, they will instinctively seek the uncourtly figure of that forest-born LIBERATOR, who by one glorious edict restored to humanity all the divine equalities enfeoffed upon it when of one blood all the children of men were made, and thus incorporated into harmonious fraternity all the estranged and repellent complexions of mankind. With reverent and grateful hearts they will pour their choicest frankincense at his feet, crown with unfailing amaranth the brow, and by eulogy, statue, column, and obelisk, and every aid to enduring remembrance, transmit to new and ever-rising futurities the irradiated name, of the first President of the regenerated Republic, that martyr to liberty and law, whom on this shore and border of time's immensity we deplore to-day,— ABRAHAM LINCOLN." *

God gave this man, whom we "delight to honor," to the world for a high and holy work: God has taken him up to the society of the sin-freed and rejoicing ones of all nations and of all time, when he had accomplished his mission; and every loyal and every Christian heart must add, "Blessed be the name of the Lord!"

* Hon. H. C. Deming.

www.ingramcontent.com/pod-product-compliance
Lightning Source LLC
LaVergne TN
LVHW011205110826
845150LV00006B/1333

* 9 7 8 1 4 2 5 5 1 8 4 4 8 *